The Alamo
An Illustrated History
by
George Nelson

Church of the Alamo. Texas.

Edited By Alicia Beigel Pais, Phd.
Aldine Books

Second Revised Edition

Published by Aldine Books

HCR 32-109
Uvalde, Texas 78801
830-232-5736
www.gnelsonstudio.com

Printed in the United States of America
by Clarke Printing Company, San Antonio, Texas

Publisher's Cataloging-in-Publication

Nelson, George S.
  The Alamo: an illustrated history/ by George Nelson.--1st
    ed.
      p.cm
      Includes bibliographical references.
      ISBN: 0-9659159-0-5

    1. Alamo (San Antonio, Tex.) 2. Alamo (San Antonio, Tex.)--
Juvenile literature.   I. Title.

F394.S2N45-1998   976.4'351

Alamo Drawing on previous page:
By Seth Eastman 1848, From the Peabody Museum, Harvard University

The Alamo
An Illustrated History

TABLE OF CONTENTS

Acknowledgments

A book of this scope involves the direct help of many persons and institutions over many years. Special thanks and acknowledgment must go to:

- Pleas McNeel who helped layout the book on his computer from a pile of pictures and an idea in my head.
- Ralph Pais of Clarke Printing was absolutely essential in making it possible for this book to make it into print. His experience, skill and kindness provided the ways and means necessary to making this a reality. Also, the staff of Clarke Printing deserves special thanks for working with me to create this book.
- Carlos G. Duran, who reshaped the Second Edition with his computer graphics expertise.
- My parents, Jack and Emma Nelson, were constant sources of love and encouragement.
- Special thanks to Kathy Herpick and the staff of the Daughters of the Republic of Texas Library at the Alamo for their help.
- Dorothy Black, head guide at the Alamo Shrine, provided crucial input and encouragement.
- Tom Shelton and the staff at the Photo Collection of the Institute of Texan Cultures was generous with their time.
- Old friends, Anne Fox and Wayne Cox of the Center for Archaeological Research at the University of Texas at San Antonio provided much needed feedback on my bird's-eye view reconstructions. Wayne Cox also provided me with information dealing with the stonemason Tellos and his standoff at the Alamo in 1744.
- Kevin Young generously supplied data on the civil war period and Gen. Andrade's occupation of the Alamo.
- Dr. Thomas Guderjan gave permission to use a drawing of a ten thousand Plainview Point found during 1995 Alamo well excavation.
- Ben Huseman at the Amon Carter Museum shared a photo of Alamo Plaza he had found at the U.S. Army Art collection in Washington, D.C.
- Aden Benavides shared his important discovery in the Old Spanish Missions Research Library at Our Lady of the Lake University, of the record of the sculptor Jesus Gonzales, who carved the entrance of the Church in 1767.
- Gary Napper and Jack Nelson aided the author in translation of Spanish documents.
- Craig Covner for sharing his finds of Seth Eastman's two 1848 drawings he located at the Peabody Museum at Harvard University. (pgs. 69 and 73)

PICTURE SOURCES

Amon Carter Museum
Benson Latin American Library, UT Austin
Center for American History, UT Austin
Center for Archaeological Research at UTSA (CAR)
Daughters of the Republic of Texas
       Library, the Alamo (DRT)
Institute of Texan Cultures Photo Collection (ITC)
John Carter Brown Library, Brown University
McNay Art Institute
Museum of New Mexico
National Archives, Washington D.C.

Newberry Library, Edward E. Ayer Collection
Peabody Museum, Harvard University
Rochester Historical Society
San Antonio Public Library, Texana Collection
St. Mary's University, Archaeology Program
Thomas Gilcrease Museum
Texas Parks and Wildlife Department
Texas State Library
University of the Incarnate Word, J.E. and L.E. Mabee
       Library, De Zavala Papers.
U.S. Army Art Collection, Washington D.C.
Witte Museum

Introduction
to First Edition 1997

The world famous battle of 1836 overshadowed the Alamo's rich history before and after that event. The adage that a picture is worth a thousand words explains the author's approach to the Alamo. A survey lasting over 25 years was made by the author, reviewing collections of old Alamo maps and pictures located across the U.S., Mexico, Spain, and England. The following is a chronological compilation of old eyewitness maps and pictures documenting the nature of the Alamo over time. Included is a brief chronology of old archival records, eyewitness descriptions, and accounts of life at the site. A large number of books, articles, films, and art has been made pertaining to the famous battle of March 6, 1836; therefore, detailed coverage of the Battle of the Alamo is not the focus of this book. Please refer to the sources at the back of the book for coverage of weapons, uniforms, tactics, and personnel of the Battle of the Alamo. The six color bird's-eye views painted by the author are provided to aid the reader in visualizing the layout of the Alamo in periods when no eyewitness views are available. These are best-guess reconstructions based on data contained in this book. They, of course, are not perfect and represent compromises with conflicting data. The 1836 period is one of the most difficult to reconstruct because many of the facts are imperfectly documented. Anyone who writes a book about the Alamo invites a firestorm of controversy, as well as risks offending at least one, if not several, partisan factions. The Alamo is a real place with a real history; it has a unique series of twists and turns that reflect its own life story. By using a visual approach, it is intended that the reader can explore the Alamo in a more in-depth way. The ultimate goal of this book is to encourage a deep love and appreciation of the site. Hopefully, this will lead to enhanced protection, research, and interpretation of the Alamo.

George Nelson, 1997

Introduction
to Second Edition 1999

This book underwent a major evolution from the first two printings. The overwhelming popularity and demand for the work is both personally satisfying and allows for continuous revising and upgrading of the material contained in this study. The major change is the movement of the color bird's-eye views of the evolution of the Alamo site to the front of the book. This allows for the consolidation of the archival documentation, historical maps and pictures into a unified, chronological narrative of the sources used to produce the color bird's-eye views.

This second edition includes never before published drawings by Seth Eastman, discovered by Craig Covner at Harvard's Peabody Museum. Old images and text from historical records expand the narrative.

When first organized, this book was over one hundred and sixty pages. Many images and documents which shed light on the colorful and controversial history of the wonderful place were not used due to space limitations. Numerous maps and pictures gathered over the years were painfully edited out of this edition. Undoubtedly, there are important maps, pictures, and descriptions of the Alamo hidden away in attics, basements, and even museums and libraries. I intend to continue to search for this information, revise, and add new images and data, to enhance future editions of this work. Hopefully, this work will bring to light new data and continue to spark expanded research into the evolution of the Alamo through time.

George Nelson, 1999

Bird's-Eye Views of the Evolution of the Alamo

The following collection of bird's-eye views are presented so the reader can review the development and evolution of Alamo Plaza over a period of more than two-hundred and fifty years. Included are seven, double page, color paintings by the author. These reconstructions represent over thirty years of research, and reflect many changes of layout and detail which were necessary as new information was discovered .

My goal is to present the Alamo's evolution clearly and accessibly. After producing bird's-eye views from all four directions, the final perspective of the painting is as if the viewer is looking northeast. This allows for the world-famous Church of San Antonio de Valero, the Alamo, to be a constant reference point. Layout of buildings, construction techniques, and materials, together with land use, roads, and vegetation patterns change over time as human needs and events dictate. The dynamic sweep of history over this one piece of earth is reflected when the bird's-eye views are combined with the old lithographs and photographs. The inconsistency of eyewitess accounts and maps does not allow for a completely accurate visualization of this ever-evolving place at the time of the legendary battle of 1836.

A collection of records, maps, and pictures follow the bird's eye views, presenting the accounts used in production of the paintings, while reviewing the colorful, complicated epic saga of this ancient place known as the Alamo.

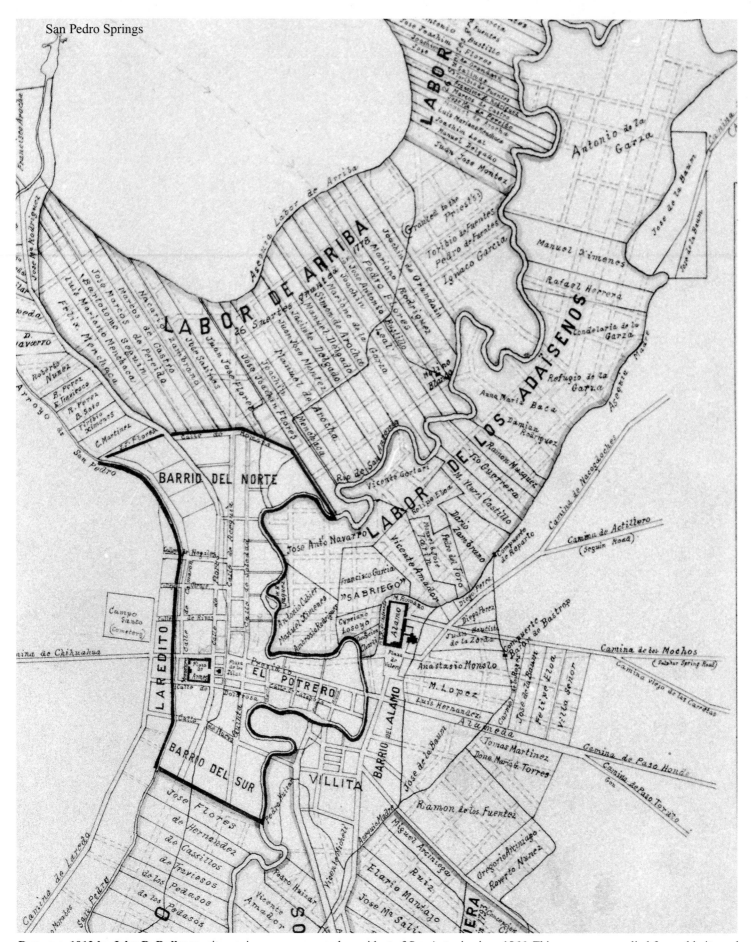

San Pedro Springs

Drawn c. 1912 by John D. Rullman, city engineer, surveyor and a resident of San Antonio since 1866. This map was complied from old city and county maps, and maps and information from private citizens. This map was used to lay out the roads, fields, and irrigation canals on the following reconstruction of San Antonio de Bexar, 1836. Center for American History, UT Austin.

2

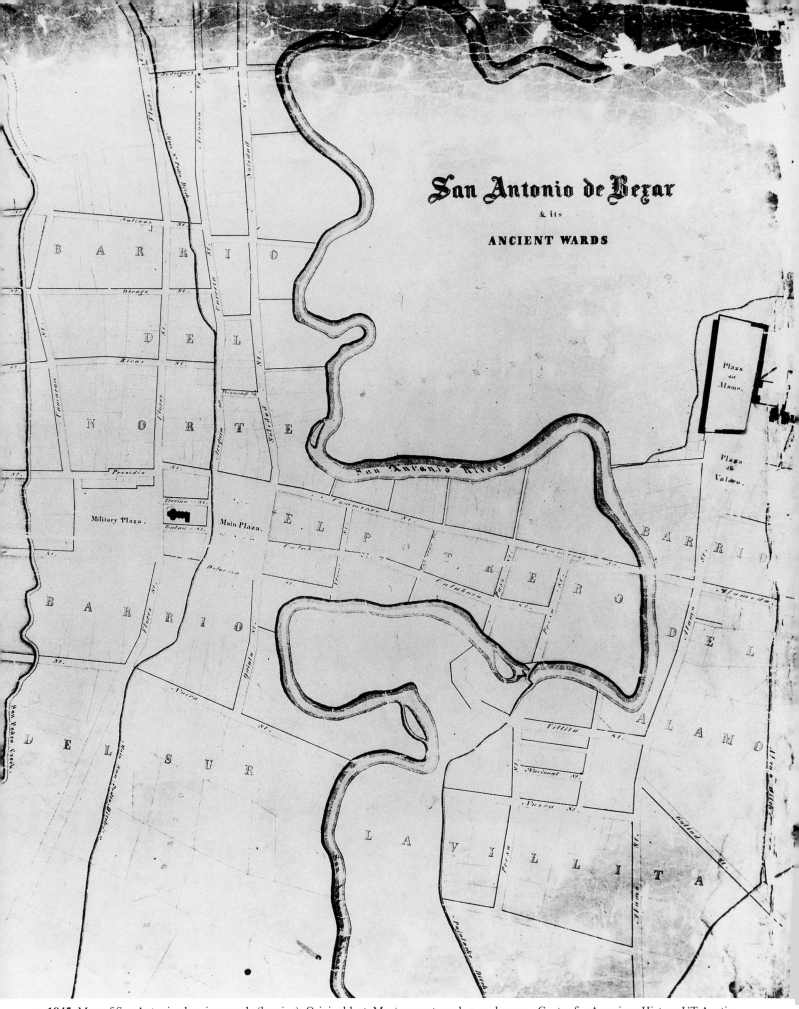

ca. 1845, Map of San Antonio showing wards (barrios); Original lost. Most accurate early map known. Center for American History UT Austin.

3

SAN ANTONIO DE BEXAR 1836   A-THE ALAMO   B-PLAZA DE VALERO   C-ALAMEDA   D-EL POTRERO   E-PLAZA DE ISLETA
K-DE LA GARZA'S HOUSE   L-VERMENDI'S HOUSE   M-ZAMBRANO'S ROW   N-GOVERNOR'S PALACE   O-LA VILLITA   P-COS HOUSE

F-PLAZA DE ARMAS G-MEXICAN REDOUBTS 1835 H-SAN FERNANDO CHURCH I-SANTA ANNA'S QUARTERS J-PRIEST'S HOUSE
Q-QUARTEL RUINS R-MOLINO BLANCO S-LA QUINTA T-MEXICAN BATTERIES 1836 U-FUNERAL PYRE V-REBEL BATTERY 1835

Alamo Plaza 1997 A. Alamo Church B. Long Barracks Museum (Convento) C. Cenotaph D. Post Office E. Emily Morgan Hotel F. Alamo Giftshop

G. Wall of History   H. DRT Library   I. Alamo Hall   J. Menger Hotel   K. Plaza de Valero   L. Site of Galera   M. Mission Indians Quarters

G

F

D

ca. 1745

MISSION SAN ANTONIO DE VALERO

A - FIRST STONE CHURCH COLLAPSED

B - TEMPORARY ADOBE CHURCH

C - PRIEST QUARTERS (CONVENTO)

D - TEMPORARY INDIAN QUARTERS

E - ADOBE INDIAN QUARTERS

F - IRRIGATION DITCH

G - IRRIGATED FIELDS

H - PEACH AND WILLOW TREES

 I - CEMETERY

ca. 1785
MISSION SAN ANTONIO DE VALERO
A - UNFINISHED SECOND STONE CHURCH
B - TEMPORARY ADOBE CHURCH
C - CONVENTO WITH TWO STORY ARCHED CLOISTER
D - ADOBE INDIAN QUARTERS WITH ARCHED PORCHES
E - GRANARY
F - TEXTILE WORKSHOP
G - GATE WITH TOWER AND THREE LOOPHOLES
I - CEMETERY
J - CHARLI HOUSE
K - PRIEST'S GARDEN

GEORGE NELSON
© 96

ALAMO 1836

A - ALAMO CHURCH
B - CONVENTO (LONG BARRACKS)
C - BURNT HOUSES OUTSIDE THE ALAMO
D - EARTHWORK DEFENDING MAIN GATE
E - GALERA
F - JAIL
G - KITCHENS
H - CIRCULAR TRENCHES AND STOCKADE
I - DAMAGED NORTH WALL
J - BATTERY WITH RAMP CALLED CONDELLE
K - BATTERY CALLED TERAN
L - FALLEN TREES
M - HORSE PEN
N - COW PEN WITH LATRINES
O - PONDS OF WATER
P - MEXICAN SIEGE BATTERY
Q - TREVIÑO HOUSE
R - WELL (LOCATION UNCLEAR)

ca. 1842
THE ALAMO
A - RUINED CHURCH
B - OLD CONVENTO
C - GALERA (Low Barracks)
D - REBUILT CHARLI HOUSE
E - REBUILT TREVIÑO HOUSE
F - REBUILT MEXICAN HOUSES
G - FORMER OUTLINE OF ALAMO WALL

THE ALAMO ca. 1861
A - CHURCH WITH NEW ROOF USED
    AS U.S. ARMY WAREHOUSE
B - CONVENTO WITH NEW ROOF USED AS
    ARMY WAREHOUSE
C - CORRALS FOR ARMY HORSES AND MULES
D - HAY YARD
E - BLACKSMITH SHOP
F - CARPENTER SHOP
G - MAVERICK HOMESTEAD
H - SAM MAVERICK'S SUBDIVISION "ALAMO CITY"
I - GALERA (FORAGE HOUSE)
J - MARKET HOUSE
K - NEW PEACH ORCHARD
L - TREES ALONG IRRIGATION DITCH
M - ORDINANCE STOREROOM

Detail Alamo Plaza, 1873, looking southeast, by Augustus Koch. See page 23 for similar view, 1928.

DRT.

19

Alamo Plaza (detail) 1886 by Augustus Koch.   M. Maverick Bank   S. Gernet's store

A. Alamo Church   44. Menger Hotel   R. San Antonio River   Witte Museum Collection

Alamo Plaza ca. 1880, Market house in foreground, Grenet's Store; "improvements" to Convento in background. ITC, San Antonio *Light*.

ca. 1890, From, *The City of San Antonio, Texas,* by Andrew Morrison. Panorama of San Antonio, North and Northeast from Dullnig's Tank. DRT.

22

The Alamo ca. 1900   ITC, Zintgraff Collection.

Alamo Plaza, ca. 1928; looking southeast, Post Office in foreground.   Atlee Ayres Collection, ITC.

23

AlamoPlaza ca. 1931
Photo by Jack Specht
from the blimp,
Enna Jettick.

A. Alamo Church

B. Convento
(Long Barracks)

C. Medical Arts
Building-Present
day Emily
Morgan Hotel

D. Scottish Rite
Masonic Lodge
Temple

E. Woolworth
Building

F. Post Office

(ITC)
San Antonio Light
Collection.

Alamo Plaza ca. 1940   A. New Cenotaph   B. New cleared garden   C. Gift shop behind church   D. Alamo Hall

Prehistoric Background of the Alamo

The 1836 Battle's fame overshadowed the 150 years of recorded history before, and 150 years of history after. However, by far the longest period of human occupation of the area was the over 10,000 years of Native American activities.

The Prehistoric Period

Archaeologists working in Texas over the past 60 years have carefully surveyed and excavated sites in the San Antonio-Bexar County area. Based on evidence found locally and on patterns of ancient human occupation in other parts of Texas, five broad periods of Indian occupation of the Alamo-San Antonio area have been established. Research that led to the creation of the atom bomb during World War II also provided archaeologists with a method of dating archaeological sites called Carbon-14 dating.

The Paleo-Indian Period
c. 9200 BC to 8,000 BC

At the end of the last Ice Age, about 11,000 years ago, evidence of early human hunters appears in the form of spearpoint types called Folsom and Plainview. These darts were thrown with the aid of a spear thrower- a wooden stick that increased the range and impact of the spear. At this time the main type of animals hunted were mastadons, huge long-horned bison, and giant sloths. Perhaps due to climate change as well as the Paleo-Indian hunters, these large ice age animals became extinct.

Pre-Archaic Period
c. 8,000 BC - 6,000 BC

This period was a transitional phase between the Paleo period and the later Archaic period. The large Ice Age animals appear to be extinct and new types of dart points were being produced. Large barbed points, notched and triangular, as well as stemmed dart points, like the Gower type, show up in the archaeological record.

The Archaic Period
c. 6,000 BC - 1,000 BC

This phase of human occupation is very long and represents a lifestyle that seems to be well-adapted for the local conditions.

Hunting of modern types of deer, bison, turkey, and fish, as well as gathering a wide range of nuts, fruits, and roots provided a stable food base. This period is divided by point type styles into Early, Middle, and Late Archaic.

The Late Prehistoric Period
c. 1200 AD - 1537 AD

This period was marked by the introduction of the bow and arrow and some crude pottery. Until the arrival of the bow and arrow technology, the ancient spear thrower (atl-atl) remained in use.

The Historic Contact Period
c. 1537 AD -1691 AD

The local Indians are first discovered and recorded by Spanish explorers around 1537, when Cabeza de Vaca, with two Spaniards and one Black, wandered from the Texas coast inland after being shipwrecked. He later wrote after returning to Spain from memory a book called "Naufragios" (The Castaways) some time between 1537 and 1541. Many Texan historians have attempted to retrace his route. Early versions had him passing through present day San Antonio. More recent studies suggest the group turned west and south and never made it to the San Antonio Alamo area. Be that as it may, Cabeza de Vaca recorded details of the local Indian culture, hunting, warfare, and trade conditions.

The Coahuiltecan Indians

In 1716, Father Olivares records that over fifty different bands or "tribes" were known by name in the area north of the Rio Grande to the San Antonio River. These many bands of Indians have been referred to as "Coahuiltecan" as if they were of the same language and common culture. This is likely an over-simplification. These local San Antonio-Alamo Indians begin to be impacted by new pressures around 1690. A French colony was established on the Texas coast around 1684, by La Salle who led explorations into the region. Spanish slaving raids across the Rio Grande, to provide labor for mines, and smallpox epidemics, ravaged the local tribes. Also, the Pueblo Revolt in New Mexico caused large numbers of horses to spread to the Comanche and Apache tribes. The larger Comanche tribe started pushing the Apaches south into central Texas. The local Coahuiltecans were recorded by the early Spanish as being under Apache attacks.

Possible Plainview Dart Point, found during 1995 archaeological excavation in disturbed soil that post-dates the mission period. This type of point is normally associated with the Paleo-Indian period ca. 10,000 years ago. This artifact is controversial; some archaeologists suggest it is a "Guerro" point dating much later. However, artifacts dating to 10,000 years ago have been found in the San Antonio area. (From Interim Report, 1995 Alamo Wells Project, Herbert G. Uecker and Thomas H. Guderjan. Used with permission.)

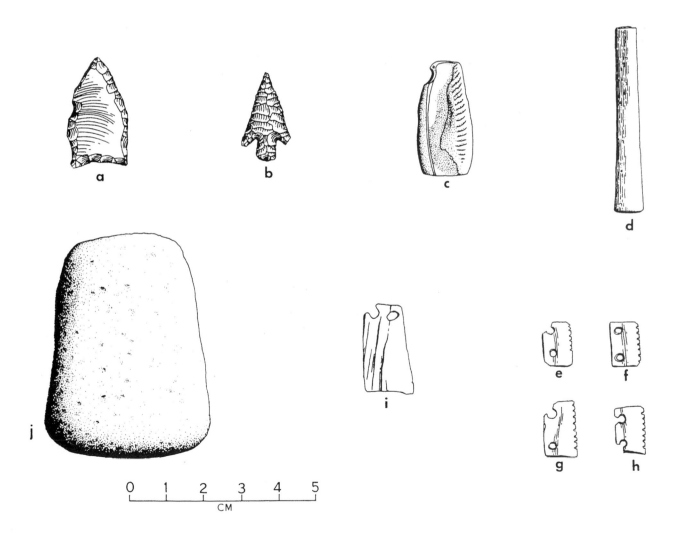

Artifacts from Alamo Plaza. a. projectile point, (tan chert); b. projectile point, (tan chert); c. Olivella shell bead; d. bird bone bead; e-h. mussel shell beads from Alamo ditch; i. mussel shell bead from Leon Creek burial site; j. basalt pestle.
Drawings by Daniel E. Fox. - Courtesy of Center for Archaeological Research, The University of Texas at San Antonio.

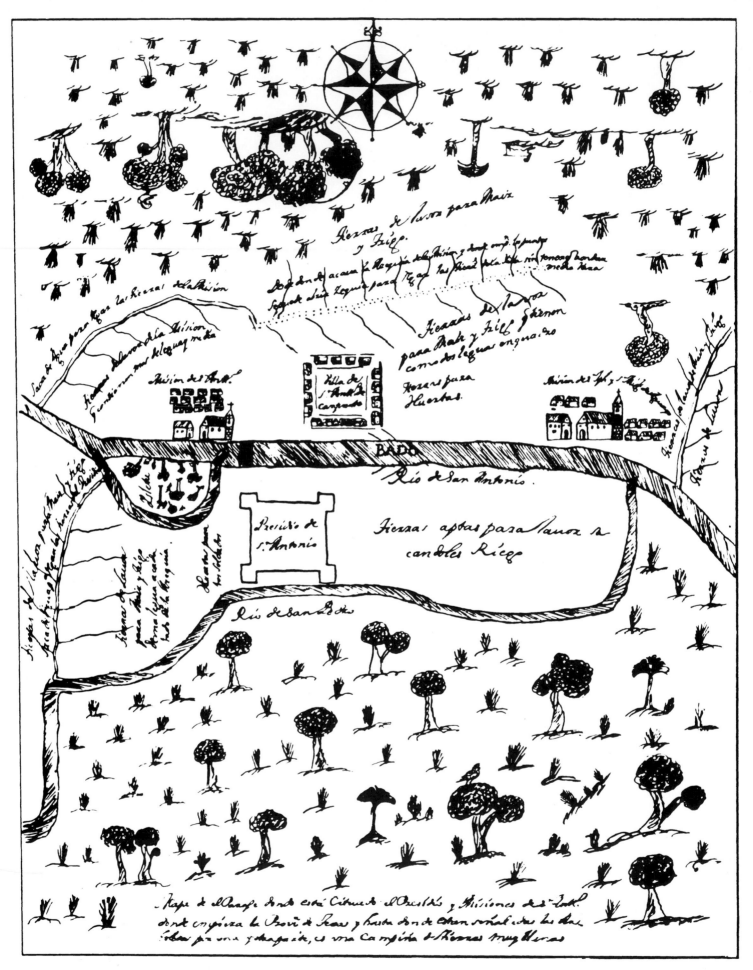

Earliest map of San Antonio, ca. 1730, map by Marques de Aguayo

ITC.

The Arrival of the Spanish

About 1690, the first official Spanish expedition to the Alamo region was in response to a French threat. A lone Frenchman named Jean Jarri was arrested west of modern San Antonio at a village called Enjen where he was the leader of local Indians. To counter French threats, Spanish missions were established in east Texas for the Tejas Indians.

First Spanish Descriptions of the San Antonio Area-1691

The earliest eyewitness descriptions of the site that would become San Antonio are contained in the diaries kept by Gov. Don Domingo Teran de los Rios and Fr. Mazanet during a visit in mid-June, 1691. The Spanish explorers continued northeast, crossing the Medina River and passing over a vast plain, "the most beautiful in New Spain." Before reaching the San Antonio River, they observed low hills covered with large oaks. The herds of buffaloes were so huge that the expedition's horses became frightened and forty stampeded. After much hard work, the soldiers rounded them up. Arriving on June 13, at the heavily wooded bank of the San Antonio River, they found a large tribe of Payaya Indians living in Rancherias (villages) at a place the Payaya called "Yanaguana." Unfortunately, the exact location and meaning of Yanaguana is unclear. The Franciscan historian, Marion Habig O.F.M., wrote that it meant "refreshing waters" but gives no source for this translation.

The 14th of June, 1691, was the feast day of Corpus Christi and the priest ordered a large cross set up as well as a brush arbor with an altar. A high mass was attended by all the Spanish and the soldiers fired many salutes, including when the host was elevated. The Payaya Indians were present and a chief of the Pacpul Indians (traveling with the Spanish) translated to them the meaning of the Mass. The next day, the chief of the Payaya, to show his appreciation, said he wished to guide them as far as the village of the Chomanes. He also ordered four Payaya men to help round up the stock and do whatever else the Spanish needed. The Spanish saw many buffaloes as they traveled northeast toward the Guadalupe River.

Visit to the San Antonio Area-1709

Eighteen years later, an expedition led by Capt. Pedro de Aguirre,

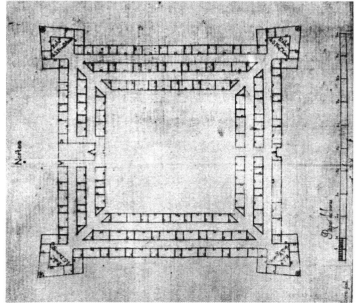

ca. 1722, Plan of Spanish fort built across the river from Mission Valero.

with Fr. Isidro Espinosa and Fr. Antonio Olivares, visited the San Antonio area and named San Pedro Springs. Fr. Antonio Olivares was taken with the idea of establishing a mission here and for the next nine years, worked to make it a reality. In 1716, an expedition led by Capt. Domingo Ramon, arrived at the future location of San Antonio with the Frenchman Louis de Saint-Denis. Both he and Fr. Isidro Felix de Espinosa kept a diary. Fr. Espinosa noted that at San Pedro Springs were poplar, elm, mulberry, and laurel trees along with grapevines, strawberries, medicinal herbs, flax two feet high, and hemp, nine feet high. He also noted alligators in the streams.

For the next nine years, Fr. Olivares wrote requests, lobbied, and pushed for permission to establish a new mission. In 1700, he had established Mission San Francisco Solano on the Rio Grande, near Presidio San Juan Bautista. Mission San Francisco Solano was the forerunner of Mission San Antonio de Valero, as it would be transferred in 1718 to the San Antonio River, along with its equipment and registry book.

In 1709, Fr. Olivares went to Spain to recruit missionaries to serve in Texas. Fr. Olivares went to Mexico City in 1716, and stayed for four months while he lobbied the new Viceroy, the Marques de Valero Baltazar de Zuniga, for permission to establish a new mission on the San Antonio River. Fr. Olivares claimed that 3,000 to 4,000 Indians would congregate there; in fact, only about 300 ever lived at the mission. To sweeten the proposal, he claimed that there was mineral wealth in the area and the new mission would be named after the Viceroy. In December of 1716, the Viceroy approved the plan and issued orders for the Governor, Don Martin de Alarcon of Texas and Coahuila, to help found the mission and a presidio (fort) on the San Antonio River.

Friction Between Fr. Olivares and Governor Alarcon

Olivares left Mexico City in December, 1716, and traveled to the Rio Grande to join the governor in preparing for the expedition to the San Antonio River. He would have to wait for almost one year. He asked the governor for the 10 soldiers the Viceroy ordered for his new mission so he could proceed to the site to begin. The governor refused. Finally, on February 16, 1718, the governor was ready with a force of seventy-two persons (including six families), and 548 horses and a cattle herd. Fr. Olivares was so frustrated with the governor that he left in his own small group of Brother Maleteta, a few Jarme Indians, and a guard of eight soldiers and traveled apart from the governor's group.

The Establishment of
Mission San Antonio de Valero-1718.

The governor's group arrived at San Pedro Springs on April 25, 1718, and Fr. Olivares' small group appears to have arrived around the same time. On May 1, 1718, the governor gave possession of the mission site to Fr. Olivares. The governor established the first site of the Presidio at San Pedro Springs on May 5. Fr. Olivares built his new mission downstream (south) from the springs. The exact location of this first site is not clear. Governor Alarcon records it was about three-quarters of a league down stream from the spring. Another description locates it "near the first spring, half a league from a high ground adjoining a small thicket of live oaks." Thatched temporary buildings were started by Fr. Olivares and three devoted

Indian companions, but the local Indians were slow to enter the new mission. Fr. Olivares accused the governor of mistreating an Indian guide who came with him from the Rio Grande. This Indian had run away and complained to the local Indians. The governor was said to have declared that if the Indians didn't come in, he would go find them and put them all to the sword. This mistreated Indian was intelligent and had followers.

However, by the winter of 1718, some Indians of the Payaya, Jarame, and Pamaya tribes had joined the new mission. Governor Alarcon returned from a trip to East Texas on January 12, 1719, and brought a bell for the new mission he found at the abandoned mission of the Tejas Indians. He proceeded to formally organize the new mission Indians into a self-governing pueblo by appointing a governor, alcaldes, and regidores, under the direction of a priest. During this first year at the first mission site, Fr. Olivares was riding across a crude bridge when his horse broke through the logs and dirt surface. The priest was thrown from the horse and broke his leg. A priest was summoned from the Rio Grande to take Fr. Olivares' confession. A soldier set his leg and Fr. Olivares recovered by spring.

1719 - The Second Mission Site

After about a year at the site on the west side of San Pedro Creek, Fr. Olivares picked a new site on the east side of the San Antonio River for the mission. It seems that this new location was chosen because of better conditions for irrigating fields by the lay of the land. The new mission began to literally take root with the digging of an irrigation ditch in January to water the new fields of watermelon, pumpkin, chile peppers, melons, grape vines, figs, corn, and beans planted in the spring of 1719. This acequia (irrigation ditch) started upstream at the ford "Paso De Tejas" from a small diversion dam. Fr. Mezquia, who was helping Fr. Olivares lay out the ditch, picked this location for the dam because "the water rises to the top of the ground and the entire work is a matter of using a plow." It seems the river water was turned into the furrow and the plow man would allow the natural flow of the water to determine the route of the acequia along the base of the ridge to the east. The second location of Mission San Antonio de Valero was located on the east bank of the San Antonio River near where Alamo Street crosses modern Commerce Street (Alameda) and St. Josephs Church. It was described as a stone two-story tower used for a chapel with priest quarters upstairs and a cluster of thatched Jacal temporary buildings. In 1727, Fr. Miguel de Paredel noted that a "small fortification" had been built two gun shots (south) from the present location (the Alamo). Everything was destroyed by a hurricane in 1724, and the final mission site was located about two blocks to the north.

1720 - Protest of Fr. Olivares against Mission San Jose

A new mission, San Jose, was proposed downstream of Mission Valero by Fr. Margil. When Fr. Olivares heard of this, he led all the mission Indians at Valero to Captain Valdes for a protest of this plan. He stated that the new mission would be too close to Valero and the Pampopas and Pastias Indians, who were to live at San Jose, were traditional enemies of the Indians of Valero.

1721 - April 1, 1721, Juan Blanco, a Negro soldier of the Texas Troops, was killed by Apaches northeast of the mission, brought to Valero, and buried.

1722 - Manuel Maldonado, a soldier from Mission Valero, died and was buried at the mission.

1724 - August, Miguel, a Payaya Indian, was killed by a blow to the head at the place they make the adobes.

1724 - The Third and Final Mission Site (Alamo Plaza)

After a devastating hurricane of 1724, a new plaza was laid out to the north.

1727 - Description by Fr. Miguel de Paredes

"Church is roofed with thatch, mission buildings are still temporary, a new friary of stone has been started. Two-hundred-seventy-three Indians live at the mission, the irrigation ditch has been dug 2.5 miles."

1728 - First Texas Cowboy

Carlos, a Ziaguan Indian, is the first known Texas cowboy. He was killed by the Apaches, 1/4 leagues from Valero and was listed as a "Vaquero" cowboy, of this mission. He was married to Barbara.

1731 - Apache Trouble

Apaches enter Mission Valero and drive off 50 burros. In January, two priests from Valero are attacked by about 50 Apaches near the Medina River.

1736 - The Feud Between the Missionary and the Governor

A bitter feud developed between Fr. Mariano of Mission Valero and the Governor Franquis. To start things off, the governor brought up the touchy subject that Mission Valero had been receiving funds from the Royal Treasury for three salaries: two priests and one lay brother, but for years there had been no lay brother at the mission. He wrote that he did not understand this type of theology.

1736 - The Battle of the Bridge

Things got worse as tempers flared. The missionary used six large logs he obtained to fix the roof of the mission church to build a bridge across the San Antonio River with mission Indian labor. This was done to allow the Spanish soldiers and settlers on the west side of the river to attend mass in the mission church. However, Fr. Mariano claimed that some Spaniards were causing trouble at the mission, bothering the Indian women and stealing things. The missionary asked the Spanish not to come to the mission. He had the mission Indians tear the bridge down, where upon the governor demanded six or eight Indians be sent him at 6 o'clock the next morning. The padre asked if they were needed for a campaign against the enemy; when told no, he said they were needed at the mission and that many were sick.

The governor ordered Lt. Mateo Perez to go to the mission with a squad of soldiers and bring six or eight Indians by force, if necessary. This was done and the bridge was rebuilt quickly under the governor's direction. He sent a message to the padre not to remove it. On Tuesday, October 17, the priest placed Indian guards at the bridge with orders, "Do not allow even the governor to pass to the Mission Pueblo." The governor, hearing of this and passing over the bridge, went into the cell of Fr. Mariano "without formalities" and, according to the padre, raised his cane to him and threatened to strike him.

1739 - The Epidemic of 1739-A terrible epidemic struck the mission in 1739, killing 116 Indians out of 300. The remaining 184 mission Indians were joined by a group of 77 Tacame Indians which deserted Mission San Jose and came to live at Mission Valero. By 1740, there were 238 Indians at the mission and the buildings were still temporary.

1744 - First Stone Church-Started On May 8, 1744, the corner stone of the new stone church was laid.

1744 - The First Standoff at Valero

On August 21, 1744, less than five months after the new stone church was started, the stone mason at the mission, Antonio Tellos, committed murder and possibly caused the new church to fall to the ground. The master mason, Tellos' girlfriend was named Roza Guerra and built her a log house. Her husband, Matias Tribino, moved to San Antonio and into his wife's new house. Matias quarreled with his wife and she threatened to have him killed. Later, the mason asked to meet him at the mission's corral near "Paso de Tejas" in the evening to get a dead calf. The husband went on to the corral and on the way back, with the calf being carried between them, Tellos suddenly pulled a gun and shot Matias Tribino. Tribino was able to ride to the house of his friend, Geronimo Flores, where he called out, "Get a confessor, I've been killed!" Flores sent for the Alcalde Don Alberto Lopez Aquady Villa Fuente, who brought the town secretary, Joseph de Arocha, to take down the statements of all involved. The investigation of the crime would do credit to Sherlock Holmes or Colombo. The mason, Tellos, meanwhile, fled to Mission Valero and barricaded himself in the church he had been building. He sent for his lover, Roza, and asked her to bring him some clean clothes as his clothes were filthy. The alcalde asked the presidio captain for help and sent some settlers and soldiers to get the culprit. The soldiers surrounded the church and were stationed at the cemetery in front. Meanwhile, the alcalde had the wounds examined by Pedro Perez who had some medical experience. There was no doctor in Texas at this time. The husband died the next morning and the wife was put in custody. A man named Mario Rodriguez talked with Tellos after he had taken refuge in the church and said Tellos claimed it was dark in the woods and he thought Matias was an Indian and shot him. After a standoff, the soldier entered the church, but found that Antonio Tellos escaped. Roza was arrested in connection with the murder of her husband.

1745 - The Battle of 1745 with the Apaches - The Mission Indians Save Spanish Fort and Town

During the night of June 30, 1745, about 350 men, women, and children of the Ypandi and Natage Apache tribes attacked the presidio (fort) and town of San Antonio across the river from Mission San Antonio de Valero. Just as the Apaches were about to set a fire, a boy spotted them and raised the alarm. The Spanish soldiers and settlers put up a desperate defense, but the Apaches attacked at three locations at the same time. Just at the point the Apaches were beginning to overrun the defenses, about 100 mission Indians from Mission San Antonio de Valero crossed the river and came to the aid of the Spanish by charging the Apaches from the rear. This broke up the Apache attack and drove off the raiders. Together, the mission Indians and the Spanish chased them to the place called Buena Vista. One of the mission Indians was an Apache captive who rejoined his people, told the chief of the Ypandi that his daughter was a hostage at Mission San Antonio de Valero, was being kindly treated, and that the Spanish wanted friendship with the Apaches. Two months after the attack, an Apache woman and boy came to San Antonio carrying a cross and claiming the Apache wanted peace.

1745 - Inventory of Mission San Antonio de Valero By Fr. Ortiz

Church: First stone church started May 1744, fell down. A new replacement was under construction. An adobe hall was being used as a temporary church. Four bells mounted to forked post in front.

Friary (Convento): Two story of stone and mortar, lower rooms are offices, upper three rooms living quarters.

Indian Quarters: Number of Indians, 311. Two long rows of adobe huts, thatched with straw, along both sides of the acequia (irrigation ditch); each row boardered by a kind of street.

Work Shops: Next to the granary was a textile shop with an open gallery and a patio with 3 rooms, 6 pairs cards, 8 combs, 6 shuttles, and 20 spinning wheels, blacksmith shop, carpenter shop, stone mason chisel and hammer.

Farm: 23 yokes of oxen, produced 1,600-1,920 bushels of corn, 96 bushels of beans, 1,000 pounds of cotton from two fields, some watermelon and pumpkins.

Earliest image of Mission Valero - ca. 1730   ITC
Detail of a map by Marques de Aquayo. Note that mission has no defensive wall and it is just a cluster of temporary buildings.

Ranch: Mission pasture land extended to the east and north, from the mission compound, 2,300 cattle, 1,317 sheep, and 304 goats.

1756 - Inventory of Mission San Antonio de Valero Church
The first church of 1744, completed with a tower and sacristy, "fell to the ground because of the poor skills of the architect." Second stone church still under construction, is made of stone quarried almost from the spot, has solidity and perfection required for beauty and to support the vaults. An old granary, 25 *varas* (approximately 97 feet long) is still used for mass. Note: At the site of the mission 1719-1724, destroyed by a hurricane, was a chapel 30 feet (11 *varas*) with a stone cross much venerated, that was equipped and sometimes still used for mass.

Friary (Convento): Two stories of stone and mortar, ground floor is guest room and various offices. Upstairs are 4 rooms and a door into the choir loft of the temporary adobe church to the south.

Indian Quarters: Mission Indians number 328; 30 houses of adobe, 20 have open porches of stone arches, some other houses of jacal (thatched huts of upright posts plastered with adobe), but new ones, like the above, were being built. An acequia ran through the plaza.

Workshop: Textile shop
Farm: 24 yokes of oxen
Ranch: 1,000 cows, 2,045 sheep, 100 horses, 50 mares

1762 - Description by Fr. Mariano Viana
The new granary and the temporary church, together with the houses of the Indians and various workshops, formed a large rectangular walk. Enclosed on the south side was a fortified gate, above it a turret with three mounted cannons.

Church: Stone church still under construction outside the Friary square. Front entrance facing west. Temporary church: Old granary 35 *varas* long (97 feet), with two altars, one with a Crucifix, 4' long

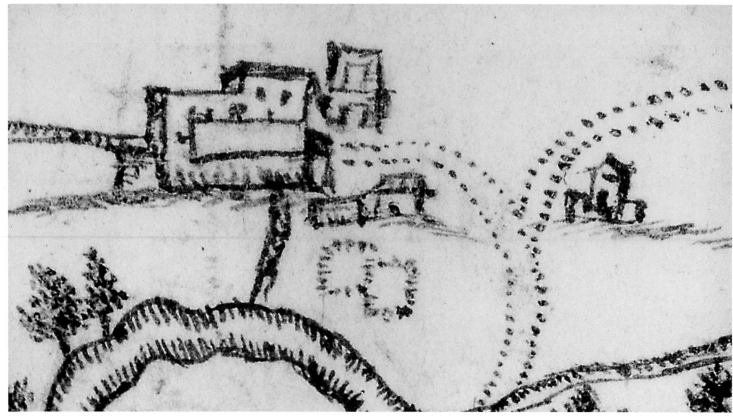

Detail of 1764 Map of San Antonio showing Mission Valero by Capt. Menchaca, Courtesy of John Carter Brown Library, Brown University.

in a niche. The other altar has an artistically clothed statue of Our Lady of Sorrow which is taken down each week for an outdoor procession where the Indians recite the Rosary. In the choir of the church there is a third altar with a statue of Jesus with benches along the sides. Four large bells. Note: The little chapel at the mission site destroyed by the 1724 hurricane was still equipped to celebrate mass.

Friary: Two story stone with private rooms, dining room, kitchen, and offices flanked by open archways facing the patio. The friary and textile shop formed a square about 50 *varas* (137 feet) long on two sides.

Textile Shop: Back of the friary in a large hall were 4 rooms and a storeroom for wool, cotton, combs, cards, and spools. Here, the Indian women make cloth and blankets of various kinds.

Indian quarters: Number of Indians is 275 (76 families), rows or tiers of houses built of stone against the walls with arched porticoes. The quarters all have doors and windows, beds raised off the ground, and chest of drawers. Household utensils were metal (corn grinding stone) comal (flat iron grill), pots and pans. On the west side outside of the plaza was flowing water shaded by willow and fruit trees that connected to the irrigation canal. Irrigation canals lined with stone ran along the east and west sides outside the two enclosures and watered the fenced mission farm.

Farm: Corn, beans, chile peppers, cotton, and some vegetables raised. Forty yokes of oxen, 30 plows, other farming tools, and 12 carts for hauling stone, timber, and supplies.

Ranch: There were 1,015 cattle, 2,300 sheep and goats, 200 mares, 15 donkeys, and 18 mules. As the ranch was a distance from the mission, a stone house 25 *varas* (69 feet) long, with 3 rooms and an arcade. There is a stone chapel also 11 *varas* (30 feet) long, a stone cross (5 feet) high, two sets of vestments for saying mass.

Note: All Indians (275) are Christian except 32 still receiving instruction for baptism. Tribes in the mission are: Jarames, Payayas,

Zanas, Apache (Ypandes), Cocos, Tops, and Karankawas. Since founding on the Rio Grande, there have been 1,572 Indians baptized, 1,247 Christian burials, and 454 marriages.

1767 - Contract With the Stone Carver

Dionicio de Jesus Gonzales was hired to carve the Ornamental Entrance to Mission San Antonio de Valero Church (Alamo Church). The contract was with Fr. Joseph Losoya and Gonzales was to be paid 1,500 pesos for his work.

1767 - March 15, Estevan Losoya, an Indian from Aquas Calientes, died and was buried. He is listed as a master mason.

1769 - Second standoff at Valero (Alamo)

Vincente Amador seeks refuge in Mission Valero after assaulting Jose Villegas. The Alcalde had sent Villegas to confiscate Amador's mare after it ate some crops. Amador stayed in Mission Valero for two months. His wife claimed it was all about the alcalde wanting the mare to raise money to spend on his girlfriends. At the end of the two month standoff, Amador gave himself up to the alcalde and was cleared, paying court costs.

1772 Inventory of Mission Valero by Fr. Pedro Ramirez

Pueblo - This pueblo is made up of 5 rows of houses. Each row has 3 houses and each house is 8 *varas* long with a door facing east and a window facing west. These houses have corridors or porches with stone arches for lighting and comfort of those who live here. Two other houses are located away from those mentioned. Although they do not have porches, they are well built for protection against the rain and wind.

The Tribes comprising this pueblo are the follows: (1) Lipanes, (2) Sanas, (3) Muruames, (4) Copan, (5) Payayas, (6) Karankawas, (7) Garames, (8) Yerbipinmes, (9) Pacuaches, (10) Papanac. The total number of persons from this mission are 53; absent neophytes, 73; for a total of 126. (The absent Indians had gone to the mission ranch and refused to come back)

Farms - This said pueblo or mission has 3 farms, each about a league long; all 3 are fenced in with poles and there is plenty of irrigation by means of a deep irrigation ditch which receives water almost from the very origin of the river and runs it in divisions throughout the areas of the said fields. One of the farms is presently planted in late corn, which is now ripe. According to a fair estimate, it should yield more than 400 fanegas. 52 plowshares for farming and 40 sickles. About 18 or 20 leagues from this pueblo, the pueblo has a ranch called La Mora which, even though it is not inhabited because of the unjust hosility of the pagans, according to a fair estimate, has from 4,000 to 5,000 cattle. The said ranch has 3 stone houses of sufficient size with good wooden roofs for every comfort.

About 3 or 4 leagues from the mission there is a large number of cattle pastured from which the pueblo is kept supplied with its weekly ration from Mount Galván.

Small Livestock - 253 mutton sheep, 1,503 goats, and 80 hogs.

Horses - 25 broken horses, 3 - 2 year old colts, 9 - 2 year old fillies, 10 young from this branded herd.

Herd - 2 broken mules and one unbroken. 33 brood mares, and 2 branding irons and a leather stap.

Workshop - Here there are, first of all, 14 sets of heddles, 13 combs, 2 1/2 pounds of mesh cloth, approximately one arroba of woolen yarn, some large scales for weighing cotton, a scale with its ball, about 24 arrobas of cotton a little of which is combed. A chest with about 12 pounds of cotton thread.

Spinning Room - Here there are a loom and 2 spinning wheels.

Wool Room - Here there are about 25 arrobas of wool. 2 worn but serviceable harnesses and some that are not. 7 sets of cards for carding wool. 14 burlap sacks. 10 pairs of shearing scissors for wool.

Forge - This room is about 7 or 8 varas long with a corresponding height and width. It contains a table with an anvil of two beaks, an anvil 7 arrobas in weight with its block. Two vises, 2 pinchers, and a mallet. 3 hammers, a drill with its bit , a bevel, a screw plate with 5 screws, 3 chisels, 3 punches for cold and 1 for hot use, a drill, 4 flat files, 2 grindstones, 2 with a medium knob, a hacksaw. Some round tongs and a grinding stone which is at the door of the forge. 4 adzes. 2 repaired planes and implements of various kinds. 4 large saws and 2 small ones. 1 iron mold for making tiles. One paring chisel, 10 large drills, and 8 small ones. Three or four arrobas of nails, 4 iron winches, 8 picks for working stone. 1 large iron mallet for the quarries, 10 chisels, large and small, 5 shovels for masonry work. 16 crow bars for quarrying stone. 5 plumbs and some level used in masonry, 7 carts, and about 150 beams for roofing or for timbers.

Utensils - The families living in the houses of the said pueblo have the following utensils for their use: 11 grinding stones, 9 pots, 10 grills, 5 copper pans.

Clothing - This past month of September of the present year 1772, each Indian was given the following items: shirt, breeches, a long heavy pull-over made of wool, breeches of material made in Queretaro, a hat, shoes, a large knife, an awl, and a rosary. In addition, the superintendent and the fiscal each received a cloak make of material from Quertaro, a shag garment lined with Rouen linen, a shirt of the same fabric, and a hair band. The Indian shepherd or herdsman was given an extra cloak of heavy Quertaro material.

The jackets, to be presented to the council members at the next meeting in 1773, are finished and kept in the cell of the missionary who administers to the temporal needs. During the above-mentioned month, each Indian woman was given the following: a blouse, white woolen skirts, flannel skirts, a blanket, a hair brush, necklaces, earrings, pendants, a plate, a cup, a basket, a long shawl, except two women who already possessed shawls of a better quality. . . .two sets of shackles to punish the delinquent Indians.

Room with salt and chile - Here, there are about 50 fenegas (bushels) of salt. Nine large old kettles with some cracks in them. An iron anvil weighing about 4 arrobas. A large copper jug for candle wax. Another one that is no good. Various large old utensils, most of them no good.

Church - The church is 35 *varas* long and 9 wide, all of Tuscan workmanship. It has a transept and a vary large sacristy, 12 *varas* long and 5 (r) wide. The facade is adorned with demi-relief and the arches must be the arris type.

Facade - The principal facade of the entire building is very beautiful and of Tuscan workmanship.

The one in the sanctuary is already completed. The 4 principal arches of carved stone serve as a foundation to support the dome. Two other arches completed in the canon (gallery), and the one for the choir loft. One of the arches for the gallery still has to be built.

The lavatory with the carved font is completed. The said lavatory is vaulted and has a great deal of light. It is 6 *varas* long and 4 wide. The baptistry, other rooms, and the anteroom have the same dimensions, are completed, and are also vaulted. They have carved doors and windows. Over the latter are the springers for two towers which the said church will have. Three small cases of glass for the windows in the dome of the new church.

At the present time, it is 9 *varas* high with 4 main collateral columns and 4 niches. In 2 of the latter are the statues of our Holy Fathers, St. Francis and St. Dominic. These statues are very devotional and are more than a *vara* high. Above the said niches are 2 others, carved but not completed. They still lack the columns and the 2 images of St. Clare and St. Margaret of Cortona. One of them is almost finished, and there are many other parts for the third section, which will be completed with a statue of Our Lady of Immaculate Concepcion with a fitting niche according to the designer's plan.

Sacristy - This is a room 12 *varas* long that has cross vaults, is well-plastered and white-washed, and has 2 carved stone doors. One serves as its entrance way and the other leads into the transept of the new church. There are 2 beautiful glass windows with wire gratings.

It also has another window that is larger and has shutters and an iron grating. Since the new church is not yet finished, the said sacristy is used as the church and has the following furnishings:

Kitchen - Here there are 3 copper skillets, 2 iron pots, 1 iron spoon, a mortar with its pestle, a metal pot for boiling, and 5 metal dishes.

Since the new church is not finished, nor the towers in which the bells will be placed, the bells are hanging from 2 poles and a forked pole placed upright next to the granary. They are as follows: 3 large bells of 15 to 18 arrobas apiece. Two small bells weighing 5 to 7 pounds each, one of which is broken. Two other small ones, one weighing from 5 to 7 pounds and the other from 8 to 10 pounds.

Living Quarters for the Missionaries - The building, which is generally called the mission by some, the convent by others, is a patio in the center of which is a well with its curbstone and arch surmounted by an artistically carved stone cross. The patio is 30 *varas* square with an arched cloister. Four sides of the cloister are roofed for the lower floor, which gives an idea of the lower cloister, though not perfectly, because the part facing east is not completely roofed. The walls of the sides facing west and south being made higher with their corresponding roof form the part that we call the upper cloister, though at present, as one can see, it is merely half of an upper cloister. The principal entrance is at the west side. It is sufficiently larger, being 9 *varas* long and 5 wide. It comprises two

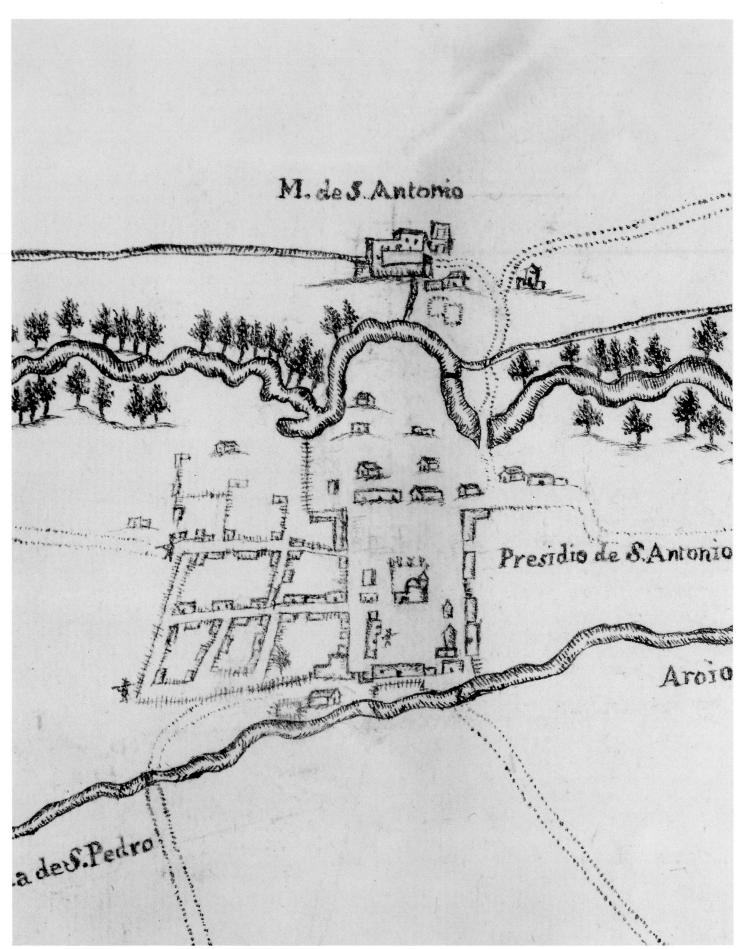

M. de S. Antonio

Presidio de S. Antonio

Aroio

a de S. Pedro

1764 Detail of San Antonio and Mission San Antonio de Valero (upper center) by Luis Antonio Menchaca, Commander of the Presidio.
Courtesy John Carter Brown Library, Brown University.

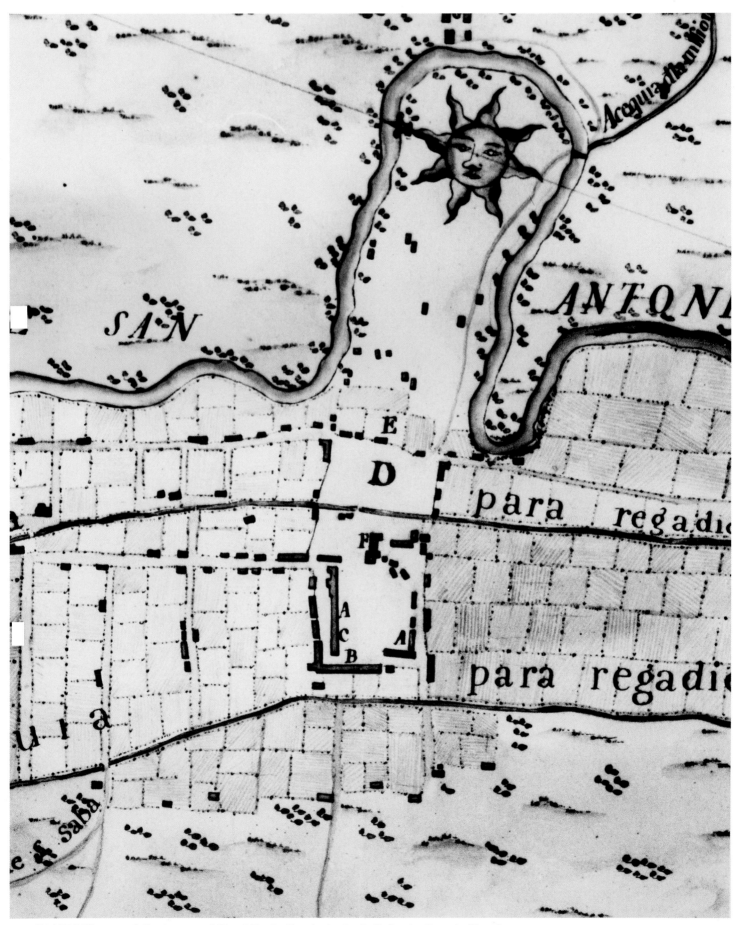

Detail, 1776-78 map of the town and Presidio de San Antonio de Bejar by Jose de Urrutia.
Explanation - a. Houses of the Presidio (fort) **b.** Captain's house **c.** Officer of the Guard **d.** Town Plaza **e.** Royal houses **f.** Church **g.** Mission of San Joseph (incorrect, should be Valero (Alamo). Unfortunately, the mission compound is left off the map, only some small huts outside on the west side are shown. Original in British Museum, detail courtesy Museum of New Mexico

rooms of the same size: one used as a workshop and the other as an office. Above these rooms are three rooms of the same dimensions. One is a guest room, and the other two are the living quarters for the missionaries. The one designed as a guest room is almost uninhabitable because part of the roof is propped up. The next room is the missionary's and is in keeping with a spiritual life. It contains the following:

A framework made of boards that forms a kind of alcove or bedroom to protect one from the cold and also serves as a retreat for study. Next to the framework or bedroom are several small chests and jars in which to keep the medicines and medicinal herbs for the use of the sick religious, should there be one at these missions. The said cell has a bedroom formed by a dividing wall in the center of which is a door with its key. In the said bedroom there is a bedstead with a mattress, 2 blankets, and 2 pillows with their pillow cases. Two copper chambers, one large and one small.

In the said alcove there is a trapdoor through which one descends to one of the rooms parallel to the main entrance. This is an office and contains the following: six small saluting guns for use on the feast day of the pueblo's patron saint. Fifteen pounds of powder, approximately, and some bullets. Three muskets and 5 shotguns.

1773 - Town council recommends Mission be secularized

Spanish refugees from Los Adaes are driven out of east Texas by the French and arrive in San Antonio. Sixty families are in need of land to live on. The town council recommends Mission Valero be secularized and some of its lands be given to help these poor refugees.

1779 - In June 1779, Governor Ripperda orders Mission Valero's secularization. The land, buildings, livestock, and crops are to be distributed to the mission Indians, Adaesanos and other landless Spanish settlers. Governor Cabello fails to carry out this order.

1781 - A second order to secularize Mission Valero is not obeyed by Governor Cabello. No reason is given.

CENSUS
December 31, 1783
San Antonio de Valero

Men	Women	Boys	Girls
49	35	36	29

1785 - First Grant of Mission Valero land

Grant of Land to Pedro Charli, the Mission Carpenter, Barber and Sacristan, Fr. Francisco Lopez granted the southwest corner room of the Mission Valero compound along with a house and plot of land outside the southwest corner. The plot of land was the location of the missionaries' vegetable gardens. Pedro Charli was to care for the padre's garden. His wife was to wash the padre's clothes. The southwest room he was given was used as a carpenter's shop and was described as a jacal.

1786 - The Beginning of the Tourist Hotels on the River Walk

A huge jacal is built to house visiting Indians across the river from Mission Valero. The interpreter, Andres Courbiere, donated the site on the Potrero (oxbow bend) on the river because the Indians liked to bathe every day. It was 144 feet long, 15 feet wide, and divided into four 36 foot rooms. Five different tribes could have their own private quarters. Local people were paid to cook and clean and one or two soldiers watched over their needs. Food and firewood was provided. This appears to have been a forerunner of the "River Walk Hotels" that cater to modern visitors to San Antonio.

1789 - Description of Mission Valero by Fr. Lopez

A wall of stone and mud enclosed an almost square "about 300 paces from the center." This rampart is the back wall of Indian quarters.

Church - A large nave built only to the cornices and a transept built only to the dome of the sanctuary. The beautiful facade of sculptured stone built only to cornice height. Because of lack of Indians and other reasons, it cannot now be completed. The value of the church and sanctuary is at least 20,000 pesos with 8,000 pesos for the furnishings and ornaments.

Sacristy - The adjoining friary now serves as the temporary church. It is on the north side of the new church. Both are of stone and mortar with arched roofs.

Friary - On the east side of the mission square is an adequate living quarters for the missionary and officers of the community of stone and lime, with good roofs, doors, windows and locks.

Indian Quarters - Fifteen or sixteen houses built against the mission wall are ample for lodging the Indians. Nearly all are covered with wood and mortar for protection from rain. They have hand-carved wooden doors within iron locks and keys.

Granary - Stone and lime, can hold 3,200 bushels of corn plus beans, etc.

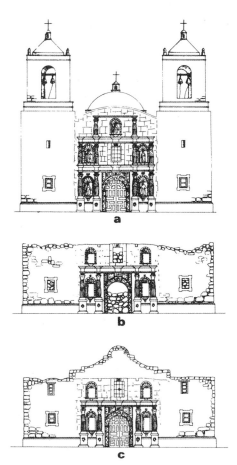

Reconstructions of the facade of the Mission Valero Church (Alamo) By Jack D. Easton.

A. "Suggested Original Elevation" of Facade church showing generalized reconstruction of how the church was designed to look when completed with a three-level baroque retable. Bell towers and dome never finished.

B. Facade of the church at the time of the battle of 1836.

C. Facade of the church as repaired by U.S. Army in 1850.

From Jack D. Eaton, Excavations at the Alamo Shrine, 1980 - Courtesy of Center for Archaeological Research UTSA.

Secularization of Mission Valero

1793 - A Detailed Inspection of Mission Valero.

Governor Munoz appointed Antonio Salazar, master mason, and Pedro Huizar, carpenter, to report on the mission buildings. Vicente Amador and Joaquin Flores, residents and officers of the Cabildo of the Villa de San Fernando, assisted them.

The home of the missionary was found to be a solidly built stone house, measuring twenty-two and three-quarters by twenty-two and one-half *varas*. The north and the south wings were both two stories high and divided by a hall. Each wing had five rooms which served as cells, each cell being five by four *varas*. These two tiers of cells were in need of repair because the flat roof was full of holes.

The west wing also had a second story and a corridor. On the first floor there was an office, and four rooms, longer than those described, and a small room at the base of the stairway. On the second story were three cells. The roofs were partly rotted and needed repairs. In the middle of the patio, there was a well with a stone superstructure, arch, and bucket. On the east side of the irregular rectangle of the mission ran a wall from north to south, one hundred and seventy-five *varas* long. The south wall ran east and west for fifty-eight *varas*. Both walls were three *varas* high and three-quarters of a *vara* thick, made of stone, adobe, and mud. Half the north wall was in ruins. The main gate that led to the plaza through the south wall measured five *varas* in width and four *varas* in height. Within the enclosure completed by the church and mission buildings were the houses of the neophytes. Adjoining the Padres' quarters was a building thirty *varas* long, five wide, and seven high, with adobe floor. Which was used as the barn. The roof of this storehouse was in very poor condition; only the beams were sound. A small rampart with a one-pound cannon stood near the entrance of the Padres' house. There was also a large jacal built of mud and willow wands with a straw roof, which was also being used as a storehouse at this time. Most of the Indian quarters faced the archway along the western wing. Of these, only twelve were habitable; the others were in ruins.

The church - This had not been completed. It was one hundred *varas* long and nine wide, with a transept. The type of architecture was Tuscan. The domed roof rested upon groups of columns. The group of columns in the presbyter had been completed and three others almost finished. The baptistry lacked the doors only. The central facade was a showy and impressive piece of Tuscan architecture. The first group of sculptured figures, consisting of two stone statues of St. Francis and St. Dominic, was completed.

The sacristy - This was twelve *varas* long, five high, and five wide. At this time it was being used as the church. It too had a domed roof. The walls, though not plastered, had been neatly whitewashed. There were two doors with carved stone frames. One of these led into an adjoining room eight and two-thirds *varas* by seven and two-thirds, with a wooden roof and cedar rafters. This room had a door on the north side and one on the east and two windows facing south and west. The doors had iron hooks and eyes. Its roof, like that of the rest of the building, was in urgent need of repairs.

Statues and paintings - On April 24, the inventory of the statues, paintings, and altars was made. On one of the side altars, in a glass case, was a statue of Saint Anthony holding the child Jesus in his arms. The Child wore a crown of silver. Over the main altar hung a large cross, one and a third *varas* long. On one side of the altar was a statue of the Nazarene in a purple tunic, bearing His cross. On the opposite side was a statue, three-quarter size, of Saint Joseph, with a silver crown, staff, and the child Jesus standing by his side. There was also a statue of Our Lady of Sorrows. In the adjoining room, which served as the sacristy, was another three-quarter statue of Saint Anthony. On a post outside the building was a large bell in good condition, and two others that were cracked. There were also five hundred new shingles, eighteen hewn logs, and one hundred fifty cedar rafters intended for the repairs of the roofs.

Division of the Mission Land

From the best and most fertile lands near the mission pueblos, eight *suertes* (plats), four hundred by two hundred *varas* each, were to be surveyed and set aside for the common use of the Indians. Each might plant his corn there in accord with the provisions of Law 3, Title 4, Book 6 of the Law of the Indies, ordered to be over served by Article 44 of the Ordinances of the Intendencies. Two or three additional plats of the size indicated, or as many as might be deemed advisable, were at the same time to be surveyed and set aside to provide for the future needs of the Indian community.

In addition to the communal lands for the benefit of each pueblo, similar plats were to be surveyed and assigned to each family. In the case of large families, if one plat was insufficient, two might be allowed.

Each Indian was to receive title to the land assigned him, setting forth clearly the bounds and limits of his property. This service was to be performed free of cost in the name of the King. The Indians could not, for any reason, sell, alienate, dispose of, or mortgage in any manner, the lands assigned them.

Each Indian family, widower, and bachelor, received a pair of oxen, a plow, a harrow, a hoe, and a cow with a calf. Thirty-nine persons received rations from the granary of Mission Valero intended for their supplies until the new crop was harvested.

(Note: The land plots were seven to twenty one acre in size.)

The Self-Governing Pueblo of Valero

Following the secularization of Mission Valero in 1793, the community that existed around the old mission was designated a self-governing pueblo (town), independent of the town of San Antonio de Bexar, which was across the river to the west. Vincente Amador, who once took refuge in the mission church for two months, was given mission land. Thirty citizens of the new pueblo filed a protest against the appointment of Vicente Amador a "*Juez*" (Judge) of Valero Mission. On January 21, 1793, settlers from Los Adaes, living in San Antonio as refugees from French aggression, were also granted land around the mission.

After being Mission San Antonio de Valero for about 70 years, the old walled compound was referred to as Publeo (town) of Valero after secularization in 1793. Threats to Spanish Texas along the Louisiana border caused a mobilization of Spanish military forces to San Antonio and east Texas in 1802-03. The first threat was Napoleon's French actions in Europe and Louisiana; the second a much more real threat was the purchase of Louisiana in 1803 by the U.S. This presented the Spanish (later, Mexico), with a chronic problem of illegal immigration, covert and overt military invasions. A Spanish Cavalry company of 100 men was sent in January, 1803, to San Antonio in response to this threat to reinforce the old Bexar Presidial Cavalry Company that was stationed in San Antonio since 1718. The unit's name was *La Segunda Compania Volante de San Carlos de Parras* (The Second Flying Company of San Carlos of Parras).

As if this wasn't long enough, the men were actually from a small town near Parras in southern Coahuila named San Jose y Santiago del Alamo and the name of the unit became The Second Flying Company of San Carlos De Alamo de Parras. Old Spanish military records show many variations of this long name: Company of Alamo de Parras and later, just Alamo Company.

Alamo means cottonwood tree in Spanish; Parras is a grape trellis. Some historians claim the name Alamo came from the nearby cotton trees of the Alameda. The families of the Alamo Company settled in the area south of the compound around the "Plaza de Valero" and the "La Villita" (little village) area to the south. Together with the former mission Indians and Spanish settlers, they formed a separate pueblo of about 250 people, distinct from San Antonio, with their own town officials from 1793 until 1809. After that time, they were merged with the town of San Antonio de Bexar as Barrio de Alamo. The Alamo Company had its own priest and articles for performing Mass.

1805 - The First Hospital in Texas at the Alamo

The buildup of Spanish troops in Texas to counter the threat from Anglo-American invasions from Louisiana led to the need of a military hospital. Colonel Don Antonio Cordero, Governor of Coahuila, Texas, and commander of the frontier, wrote to his commanding general, Brigadier Nemerio Salcedo, on October 19, 1805, "... I have provided, without any cost whatever, and availing myself only of a little arbitration, the equipment of a party ruined chamber in a secularized Mission of Valero as a military infirmary. I have had it provided with beds made of reeds in order to avoid the dampness of the ground. The patients of all the companies or posts who may be sent here will be placed in them under the necessary care of a nurse (male), a woman to take care of the kitchen, and guard of the company of the Alamo which is stationed at this mission. The only expense entailed will be the increase of the troops one real and a half per day to two reales, and the remuneration of the doctor and cost of medicines."

Dr. Zervan, the doctor referred to in Condero's letter seems to have been a shifty character. He had skipped bail of $40,000 in Natchez, Mississippi, put up by Robert and John Moore, and moved to San Antonio.

Dr. Zervan had an assistant or "practitioner" named Lazaro Orranti, who acted as pharmacist. The practitioner had experience in Coahuila. Dr. Zervan seems to have rubbed some folks the wrong way. On April 24, 1806, the attorney of the town council of San Antonio wrote to Governor Condero that the townspeople were very unhappy with his practice of medicine and surgery. They stated that home remedies were better and less harmful than the doctor's cures. Dr. Zervan should cease to practice his profession and any new doctor be examined by the King's Medical Board. The governor reacted by firing the town attorney.

When the American spy, Lt. Zebulon Pike, was passing as a prisoner through San Antonio in June 1807, he met "Dr. Zerbin." Pike noted Zervan had lived at Natchez, but because "of pecuniary embarrassments, immigrated to the Spanish Territories." The doctor was described as handsome in person, "but he had recently committed some very great indiscretions, by which he had nearly lost the favor of Colonel Cordero, though whilst we were there, he was treated with attention."

Another doctor, Pedro Lartique of Louisiana, was granted permission on August 7, 1806, to practice as "Master of Surgery in the class of Dentistry." He claimed 23 or 24 years of experience and promised to give medicine free of charge to people of notable poverty.

1806 - The Robbery of Texas' First Dentist by Alamo Hospital Attendant

On December 12, 1806, Dr. Lartique was robbed and a detailed investigation was done by Captain Amanqual of the Alamo Company. The dentist stated he thought the thief was the uncle of his cook, Private Felipe Gonzalez of the Alamo Company. Gonzalez was 27, single, and a *Mulatto* who worked at the hospital. Two other local men were implicated. The investigation reveals San Antonio had a pool hall and gunsmith shop, as these places were used in the alibis during questioning.

1806 - Small Pox Vaccination Comes to the Alamo

In 1805, a ship set sail from Spain to America bearing a large number of children. On the voyage, two of the children were vaccinated each week with the virus taken from the sores on the two children vaccinated the previous week. Thus, the virus was kept alive and brought from Spain to her possessions in the New World.

On April 8, 1806, the provisional governor of Texas made this report from Bexar to the Commander General: "Along with the order of Your Lordship dated the 11th of last month, I received the vial with the vaccine fluid, and the paper full of scabs of smallpox which accompanied it. The first of this month I placed twelve children — six belonging to the troops and six belonging to the settlers — in a room in the temporary military hospital. They received the operation and remained under the care of the physician until the work of transferring the matter (pus) from arm to arm was accomplished. I shall report the results to your lordship."

1806-Daniel Boone petitions to settle in San Antonio, June 11, 1806. A relative of the famous frontiersman, he became gunsmith for the Spanish military and contracted to make rifles and pistols in a gunshop near the Alamo. He moved to Texas over a land dispute in the United States. After he was killed by Indians his widow remarried Nandin Andres. At least two other Anglo Americans worked as gunsmiths for the Spanish and Mexican governments. Besides repairing guns, an Anglo American carpenter was contracted to make wooden cannon carriages.

Improvements Made at the Hospital

December 27, 1806 - After 14 months of making do with beds of reed, Governor Cordero ordered Francisco Amangual to buy lumber and build thirty beds, fully equipped. This was quickly done.

(*Brand of Alamo Company)

ca. 1804, Spanish Presidal Soldier showing how the Alamo Company may have appeared. Spanish uniforms of these troops was a short blue jacket with red cuffs and collar and knee length blue pants. This figure is shown wearing a new short version of the leather armor. The old style leather vest extended halfway to the knees. He is armed with a lance, shield, carbine, and two flintlock pistols. In cold weather they wore long blue capes. (ITC).

On September 1, 1807, Governor Cordero ordered "the construction of two rooms in the abandoned Mission of Valero, to the end that they may serve as the pharmacy of the military hospital which has been temporarily established here."

The old Spanish records contain many requests for more medicines over the years. For example, on March 2, 1808, the Administrator, Francisco Amanqual, wrote Governor Cordero that every effort was being made to get a pharmacist and the purchase of honey, snake root, and turpentine. The request was approved, and the doctor was asked to make up a list of medicines needed so they could be ordered from Mexico City.

The staff of the hospital included a doctor, pharmacist, female cooks, 1 or 2 male nurses, (later, in 1808, a third nurse was added). At times, the staff demanded more pay and would get it.

A ration of mutton soup, bread, and cigarettes was allowed each patient. At first, only soldiers were treated; later, the families of the soldiers and the townspeople of San Antonio were also treated at the cost of 1 *real* a day.

The first hospital and medical care in Texas was a semi-socialized government program in 1805.

1809 - Major Repairs to the Alamo Hospital

On May 5, 1809, Dr. Jaime Garza wrote a report recommending repairs be made to the hospital building. Local master masons, Juan Diego Velos, Juan de Dias Cortez, and Francisco Zapata were asked to "make an estimate of the material and other effects needed for said rebuilding." "Experts" were employed to examine the hospital and recommended that a new roof and gutter be added, the floors both upstairs and down be repaired, the chinks in all the walls be filled with small rocks and mortar, and 834 *varas* (about 2,500 feet) of concrete battlements be constructed and plastered with mortar. This is way too much area to just be referring to the upper walls of the old mission convent. Either the amount is a mistake or perhaps the entire mission compound wall was repaired and capped with concrete "battlements." The 1836 drawing by Sanchez Navarro shows loopholes along the top of the west wall. The master masons, who could not read, produced a detailed estimate: 2,000 barrels of lime, 820 cart loads of sand, 16,995 shingles and 12 beef hides to make leather straps for tying the scaffolds. A total bid of 5,979 *pesos*, 4 *reales* was made to do the work. The work began and all the patients were moved temporarily to the home of Widow Doña Concepción, who was to have the walls of her home whitewashed and plastered and be paid a rent of 20 *pesos* a month.

ca. 1828, Mexican Presidal soldier of Texas-The Alamo Company Soldiers may have appeared similar to this one. This figure shows that the lance, shield, and leather vest have been discarded and a stylish tophat has been adopted. Note the apron like covering of his upper legs. His carbine is covered with a fringed scabbard.   Painting by L. Sanchez y Tapia. Courtesy, The Gilcrease Museum.

January 1, 1805 Mobil Troops of San Carlos De Parras				
	Men	Women	Boys	Girls	Total
Married	54	54	47	35	190
Single	41				41
Widowed	5	6	3	1	15
Priest	1			1(?)	2
TOTAL	101	60	50	37	248

San Antonio de Valero By Dionisio Valle

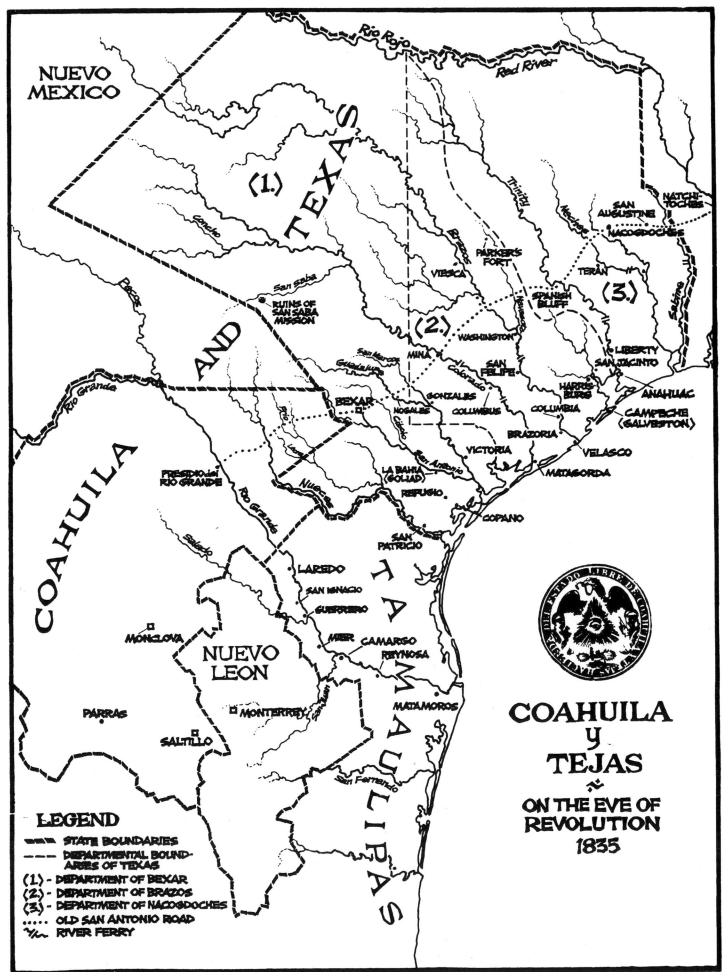

COAHUILA
Y
TEJAS
~
ON THE EVE OF
REVOLUTION
1835

Courtesy of Jack Jackson

43

Old Mexican Lookout or Watch Tower at San Antonio, Texas. 2 miles from the Alamo.

Nov 22° 184

La Garita and Powder House, by Seth Eastman, 1848. Built on a hill east of the Alamo by the Spanish, ca. 1804-1809, to guard San Antonio from feared Anglo-American attack. It was protected by an earthwork bastion with two flanking trenches. This was a site of a battle during the siege of Bexar in 1835, when Mexican Army troops marched out of the Alamo and attacked Rebel forces occupying this site. Later, the U.S. Army used the site to store ammunition and the Confederate forces occupied it as a strong point. The Spanish also built a Garita on a hill east of Santa Fe at about the same time. During the siege of the Alamo, Santa Anna's forces were stationed here with an artillery emplacement. From Seth Eastman's <u>Sketchbook</u>, McNay Art Museum.

By early 1810, the work was completed and Governor Salcedo approved payment for the reconstruction. This record of major remodeling is intriguing because it seems a wooden shingle roof was to be installed, while the 1836 Sanchez Navarro's drawing seems to show a flat roof. Perhaps it was a low pitched shed roof draining to the east. Edward Everett stated in 1847 the old flat roofs of earth and cement were torn off and replaced by a new shingle roof.

THE MEXICAN WAR FOR INDEPENDENCE 1810-1821

The Alamo was the site of much activity during the ten year war for Mexican Independence. The fort changed hands several times between Spanish Royalists and Rebels. Following Father Hidalgo's call for revolt in 1810, two rebel agents, Lieutenant Saenz and Lieutenant Escamilla, arrived in San Antonio, were arrested and jailed at the Alamo. Governor Saucedo planned to move his troops to the Rio Grande but the local soldiers resented the move and rumors spread that the barracks at the Alamo would be burnt. On the morning of January 22, 1811, retired captain Juan Bautista de Las Casas led a barracks coup, and the governor and commandant were put in jail at the Alamo. The two rebel agents were freed; however, Lt. Saenz fell out with Las Casas and joined Juan Zambrano in a counter revolution. Rebel agents, Fr. Salazar

and Ignacio Aldana, were put in jail at the Alamo, where they continued to agitate the troops to rebel against the Spanish.

In 1813, Jose Bernardo Gutierrez de Lara went to the U.S. and raised about 300 volunteers. After capturing La Bahia, his army, numbering about 800 now, marched on San Antonio. On April 1, 1813, Gov. Saucedo and other Spanish officers surrendered and were forced to march at the head of the rebel army into the Alamo. The rebel army occupied the Alamo with several hundred troops as their headquarters. The governor and other officials were put on trial for, among other things, causing Capt. Luis Menchaca to be shot, his head cut off and placed on a pike at the gate of the Alamo. Gov. Saucedo and sixteen Spanish officers were taken by a group of about one hundred mounted men composed of troops from the Alamo, Bexar, and La Bahia, as well as some American volunteers. Lead by Antonio Delgado, of the Bexar Militia and Pedro Prado of the Alamo Company, they took the prisoners a few miles south of town, slit their throats, and left them for the buzzards. August 18, 1813, Gen. Joaquin de Arredondo defeated the rebels at the Battle of the Medina and the Spanish controlled the Alamo until 1821. Around 1821, a map showing an artillery position at Valero was corrected and sent to Mexico City, how ever this map has not been located.

View from near the powderhouse by Seth Eastmen, 1848. This forms a panoramic view from the hilltop towards the town of San Antonio de Bexar. The tall trees on the left side of the picture is the Alameda. In the center is San Fernando Church, and on the right edge of the picture is the rear of the Alamo Church.

From Seth Eastman's Sketchbook, McNay Art Museum

The Mexican Army Occupation of the Alamo - 1821-1836

The old Baptismal Registry Book which the Spanish Cavalry unit had brought to Valero in 1803 was ordered closed on August 22, 1824. The Alamo Troop was identified on the registry as "Second Company of Volante of San Carlos of Parras, located at the Town of Alamo, Texas."

The Alamo is Saved for the First Time - 1825

Anastacio Bustamante

On August 25, 1825, political chief, Saucedo, wrote Governor Rafael Gonzalez asking if the stone in the old walls and mission buildings could be sold to raise funds. At the same time, the commander at the Alamo requested that the old priest quarters at Valero be assigned permanent barracks for the Alamo troops.

The issue was referred to the State Legislature which, in chronic need for money, ordered in 1827, that the rock in the walls of the secularized missions be sold for cash at public auction, the funds turned over to the State Treasurer. The new commandant of the Eastern Provinces, Anastacio Bustamante, stepped in and demanded suspension of the order as it applied to Mission Valero because he desired the old buildings be permanently used as barracks for the Alamo Company. Bustamante, who would soon become President of Mexico, was very familiar with the Alamo and had close friendships with local Texas Indians who gave him refuge during the War for Independence from Spain. He deserves the recognition as first savior of the Alamo, an honor that also belongs to Brig. General Sidney Jesup(1850), Adina DeZavala, and Clara Driscoll. In September, 1831, a ruling protected all mission churches that were to be used for religious services. Bustamante was a politcal opponant of General Santa Anna.

Alamo Company Stationed at Fort Tenoxtitlan - 1830-1832

In response to the law of April 6, 1830, intended to stop illegal immigration of Anglo-Americans, a new Mexican fort named Tenoxtilan, after the old Aztec name for Mexico City was built on the Brazos River. Under command of Lt. Col. Jose Francisco Ruiz, the Alamo Company moved to the site and built the new fort. It seems Ruiz made a wooden model of how the fort should be built and it was taken to the site to guide the workers. Conditions were harsh and desertions common. On August 22, 1832, Fort Tenoxtilan was abandoned. On September 14, the Alamo Company returned to the Alamo with their families.

The Alamo During the Texas Revolution 1835-1836

The Alamo played a central role in events during the revolution of 1835-36. It was the site of two sieges and changed hands three times during the war. The first combat and bloodshed involved the hundred cavalry troopers of the Alamo Company under Lt. Francisco Castaneda when they went to retrieve a small cannon lent to the town of Gonzales.

Siege of Bexar

General Martin Perfecto de Cos arrived in San Antonio with five hundred soldiers on October 11, 1835, to counter a rebellion that had just resulted in the shoot-out at Gonzales, about a week before. Cos set his soldiers to work fortifying the Alamo and the town of Bexar. Most of the defenses of the Alamo during the famous battle of 1836 would have been constructed by the Mexican soldiers under Cos. Trenches were dug, dirt was piled up in ramps and platforms for cannons to shoot over the walls, and a stockade was built across the open cemetery area in front of the church. Around two hundred cavalry, including the Alamo Company, and about three hundred infantry, were stationed in the Alamo during the 56 day siege of Bexar in 1835. The rebels bombarded the old fort with cannons. Deaf Smith won a bet that he could place a shot with a cannon and knock down the third and forth windows of the Alamo. Perhaps this referred to the north end of the second floor of the old covento.

After 56 days of siege, General Cos agreed to terms that allowed his troops to march away with their muskets and a 4 pound cannon. Some of the Mexican Alamo Company stayed in San Antonio. The rebel force that agreed to remain in town lost about 200 men after Johnson, Grant, Bowie, and Fannin each recruited small armies under their independent command, to pursue a plundering raid on Matamoros, Mexico. Despite pleas for supplies, money and men, Lt. Col. James C. Neill was faced with two distinct fortresses to garrison with, about 24 pieces of artillery and only 104 men left in San Antonio under his command. Neill eventually left San Antonio and the command of the rebel garrison was shared by William B. Travis and James Bowie.

January 17, 1836 - Sam Houston Wants to Blow Up the Alamo

In a letter to Gov. Henry Smith, Houston states: "I have ordered the fortifications in the town of Bexar to be demolished, and if you should think well of it, I will remove all the cannons and other munitions of war to Gonzales and Copano, blow the Alamo, and abandon the place, as it will be impossible to keep up the station with volunteers."

Letters from G. B. Jameson, Engineer of the Alamo

Bexar, January 18th, 1836
Major-General Sam Houston,
Sir: Believing that a letter will meet you at Goliad and having had more time to make a better plat of the 'Fortress Alamo' at this place having embraced this conveyance to acquaint you more satisfactorily of the condition and progress of the department, which you have so kindly assigned to me.

I am sending you herewith enclosed a neat plat of the fortress exhibiting its true condition at this time, as also an Index being duplicates of my former addressed to you at Washington, added to which is a recapitulation more explanatory, and showing the improvements already made by me.

I am now fortifying and mounting the cannon. The 18-pounder now on the northwest corner of the fortress so as to command the town and the country around.

The officers of every department do more work than the men and also stand guard, and act as patrol every night. I have no doubt but that the enemy have spies in town every twenty-four hours, and we are using our utmost endeavors to catch them every night, nor have I any doubt that there are 1500 of the enemy at the town of Rio Grande, and as many more at Laredo, and I believe they know our situation as well as we do ourselves.

We have received 100 bushels of meal and 42 beeves which will last us for two months to come, but no other supplies have come to our relief.

You have heard so much about our situation from our commander that I shall say nothing further on the subject.

We can rely on aid from the citizens of this town in the case of a siege. Seguin is doing all he can for the cause, as well as many of the most wealthy and influential citizens.

You can plainly see by the plat that the Alamo was never built by a military people for a fortress; thou (she) is strong, there is not a redoubt that will command the whole line of the fort, all is in plain wall and intended to take advantage with a few pieces of artillery, it is a strong place and better it should remain as it is after completing the half moon batteries than to rebuild it. The men I have will not labor and I cannot ask it of them until they are better clad and fed. We have now 114 men counting officers, the sick and wounded which leaves us about 80 efficient men, 40 in the Alamo and 40 in town, leaving all the patrol duty to be done by the officers and which for lack of horses has to be done on foot.

We have had loose discipline until lately. Since we heard of 1000 to 1500 men of the enemy being on their march to this place, duty is being done well and punctually; in case of an attack we will all move into the Alamo and whip 10 to 1 with artillery.

If the men here get a reasonable supply of clothing, provisions and money, they will remain the balance of the four months, and do duty and fight better than fresh men; they have been tried and have confidence in themselves.

I can give you full assurance that so far as I am concerned, there shall be nothing wanting on my part neither as an officer nor as a soldier to promote and sustain the great cause at which we are all aiming, and am at all times respectfully subject to your orders for the verification of which I refer you to my commander at this place as well as all the officers and men, I have been much flattered for my exertions at this place. I have more than one time received the vote of thanks of the whole Garrison.

I am with esteem
Your obt. Servt.
G. B. Jameson

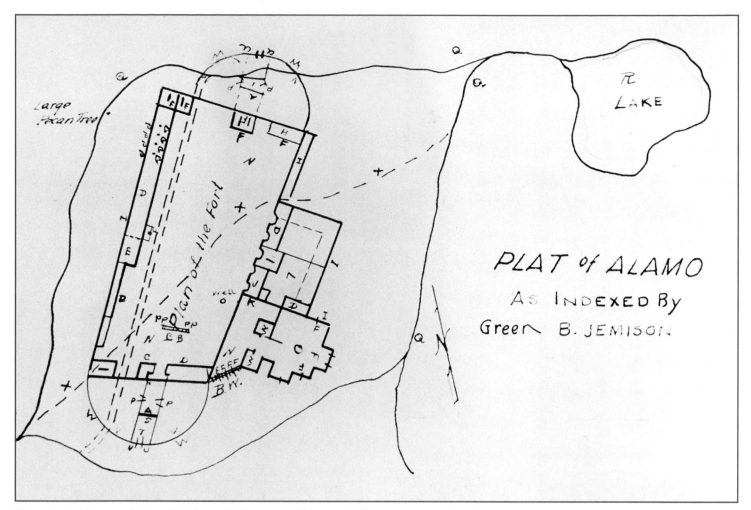

Plat of the Alamo as indexed by Green B. Jameson -This map is illustrated in Amelia Williams', "A Critical Study of the Siege of the Alamo and the personnel of its defenders." Ph.D dissertation, UT Austin, 1931. It is claimed to be a version of the original by Jameson, now lost. The accuracy of the above map is unknown and is presented only as a reference to the following index by Jameson.

A   Represents the entrance of the Alamo, covered by two cannons, p.p.

B. Temporary redoubts of stakes on end and rocks and dirt between.

C. The guard house.

D. Represents the soldiers' quarters built of stone.

E. Headquarters of the Alamo, now occupied by the wounded officers.

F. Batteries and platforms where cannon are now mounted.

G. Cannon mounted on the ground with ports in the main wall.

H. Soldiers' quarters built out of adobe houses and picketed all around as is B.W.

I.   Strong stone walls without pickets around.

J.   The hospital upstairs in a two-story building of stone; the lower story being represented by K and now occupied as an armory for small arms.

L. A large stone quarter for horses. It adjoins the church, hospitals and armory.

M. The magazine in the church, San Antonio de Valero. These are two very efficient and appropriate rooms, each 10 feet square; walls around and above are 4-feet thick.

N. All large vacancies inside the walls of the fortress. The church, San Antonio is within the Alamo and forms a part of the fortress and is marked O.

O. Alamo Church.

P.   Cannon mounted in the Alamo. The number corresponds with that of the letters. (21 may be counted).

Q. The aqueduct as around the fortress by which we are supplied with water marked with red ink.

R. A lake of water from which we contemplate supplying the fortress by ditching from one of the aqueducts laid down.

S. A pass from the present fortress to a contemplated draw bridge across a contemplated ditch inside a contemplated half moon battery as laid down on the plat.

T. A part of said ditch as well as a trapdoor across said ditch which is contemplated to be raised by a tackle from inside the half moon battery.

U. The Hinges on which said bridge is to be raised.

V. The half moon battery at each end of the fortress as contemplated.

W. Contemplated ditch of half moon battery.

X. The contemplated ditch where we wish the permanent water to pass out, erecting an arch over each place and also a redoubt for the permanent cannon in case of siege.

Jameson letters continued

I will in my next give you a plan of the Town as fortified when we took it. We have too few to garrison both places, and will bring all our forces to the Alamo tomorrow as well as the cannon. In excavating our ditches we can with perfect safety rely on a fall from the two ditches or aqueducts of at least 20 feet, consequently we can make our ditches deep enough with perfect safety, and the earth here is of such a nature that it will not wash, and we can ditch very near the half moon batteries with perfect safety. I will say all that is necessary in my answer to your official letter on this subject. In regard to the ditch, we can have a flood gate at the mouth of it which will answer for keeping in a supply of water in case of a siege, as also by raising, for cleansing the Fortress. I am too much occupied to copy these papers but I shall be able to show you by demonstration when I have nothing else to attend to that I will not be wanting in my ability as a topographical Engineer.

Respectfully, your Obt. Servt.

G. B. Jameson

Bejar - February 16, 1836

To His Excellency Henry Smith:

Sir: I have been dilatory in communicating to you the situation as well as the plans of the Fortress whereby you might know our exact defense and security in case of a siege from the enemy. But will now send you a complete plan of same, showing its situation at the time it was surrendered to us, also such improvements as we have made, and such as was contemplated to work is characterized by red ink, such improvements as we have made in erecting redoubts, digging wells and mounting cannon is characterized thus with red ink - all of which I send you for your information and that of your friends and the friends to our cause and country. But after seeing the impossibility and in policy of keeping up a strong Garrison here, I now submit a further suggestion to you as well as to the commander-in-chief which you will remark to me as you think most economical and efficient. The suggestion is to square the Alamo and erect a large redoubt at each corner supported by Bastions and have a ditch all around full of water. When squared in that way four cannon and fewer men would do more effective service than the twenty pieces of artillery do or can do in the way they are now mounted. The Mexicans have shown imbecility and want of skill in this Fortress as they have done in all things else. I have seen many fortifications in the U.S. and find that all the Interior ones are square while those of the Forts are generally circular. Taking into consideration the scarcity of tools we have done well in mounting and remounting Guns and other necessary work. If I were ordered to construct a new and effective Fortress on an economical plan, I would suggest a diamond with two acute and two obtuse angles - with few men and Guns but with a sufficient entrenchment all around. Such a fortress with projecting redoubts and Bastions would command all points.

Yr. Obt. Humble Servt.

Very respectfully

G. B. Jameson, Engineer

William B. Travis to Major-General Sam Houston - Feb 25, 1836

Headquarters, Fort of the Alamo: Sir; On the 23rd of Feb. the enemy in large force entered the city of Bexar, which could not be prevented, as I had not sufficient force to occupy both positions. Col. Bartes, the Adjutant-Major of the President-General Santa Anna, demanded a surrender at discretion, calling us foreign rebels. I answered them with a cannon shot, upon which the enemy commenced a bombardment with a five inch howitzer, which together with a heavy cannonade, has been kept up incessantly ever since. I instantly sent express to Col. Fannin, at Goliad, and to the people of Gonzales and San Felipe. Today, at 10 o'clock a.m. some two or three hundred Mexicans crossed the river below and came up under cover of the houses until they arrived within virtual point blank shot, when we opened a heavy discharge of grape and canister on them, together with a well directed fire from small arms which forced them to halt and take shelter in the houses about 90 or 100 yards from our batteries. The action continued to rage about two hours, when the enemy retreated in confusion, dragging many of their dead and wounded.

During the action the enemy kept up a constant bombardment and discharge of balls, grape, and canister. We know from actual observation that many of the enemy were wounded - while we, on our part, have not lost a man. Two or three of our men have been slightly scratched by pieces of rock, but have not been disabled. I take great pleasure in stating the both officers and men conducted themselves with firmness and bravery. Lieutenant Simmons of cavalry acting as infantry, the Captains Carery, Dickinson, and Blair of the artillery, rendered essential service, and Charles Despallier and Robert Brown gallantly sallied out and set fire to houses which afforded the enemy shelter, in the face of enemy fire. Indeed, the whole of the men who were brought into action conducted themselves with such heroism that it would be injustice to discriminate. The Hon. David Crockett was seen at all points, animating the men to do their duty. Our numbers are few and the enemy still continues to approximate his works to ours. I have every reason to apprehend an attack from his whole force very soon; but I shall hold out to the last extremity, hoping

The flag of the New Orleans Greys, from Museo National de Historia, Mexico D. F.

to secure reinforcements in a day or two. Do hasten on aid to me as rapidly as possible, as from the superior number of the enemy, it will be impossible for us to keep them out much longer. If they overpower us, we fall a sacrifice at the shrine of our country, and we hope prosperity and our country will do our memory justice. Give me help, O my country! Victory or Death!

W. Barret Travis, Lt. Col. Com.

William B. Travis to the President of the Convention March 3, 1836

Commandancy of the Alamo, Bejar: In the present confusion of the political authorities of the country, and in the absence of the commander-in-chief, I beg leave to communicate to you the situation of this garrison. You have doubtless already seen my official report of the action of the 25th ult., made on that day to General Sam Houston, together with the various communications heretofore sent by express. I shall, therefore, confine myself to what has transpired since that date.

From the 25th to the present date, the enemy have kept up a bombardment from two howitzers (one a five and a half inch, the other an eight inch) and a heavy cannonade from two long nine-pounders, mounted on a battery on the opposite side of the river, at a distance of four hundred yards from our walls. During this period the enemy has been busily employed in encircling us with entrenchments on all sides, at the following distance, to wit - in Bejar, four hundred yards west; in La Villita, three hundred yards south; at the powder-house, one thousand yards east by south; on the ditch, eight hundred yards north. Notwithstanding all this, a company of thirty-two men from Gonzales, made their way into us on the morning of the 1st. Inst, at three o'clock, and Col. J. B. Bonham (a courier from Gonzales) got in this morning at eleven o'clock without molestation. I have so fortified this place, that the walls are generally proof against cannonballs; and I shall continue to entrench on the inside, and strengthen the walls by throwing up dirt. At least two hundred shells have fallen inside our works without having injured a single man; indeed, we have been so fortunate as not to lose a man from any cause, and we have killed many of the enemy. The spirits of my men are still high, although they have had just to depress them. We have contended for ten days against an enemy whose numbers are variously estimated at from fifteen hundred to six thousand, with Gen. Ramirez Sezma and Col. Bartes, the aid-de-camp of Santa Anna, at their head. A report was circulated that Santa Anna himself was with the enemy, but I think it was false. A reinforcement of one thousand men is now entering Bexar from the west, and I think it more than probable that Santa Anna is now in town, from the rejoicing we hear. Col. Fannin is said to be on the march to this place with reinforcements; but I fear it is not true, as I have repeatedly sent to him for aid without receiving any. Col. Bonham, my special messenger, arrived at La Bahia fourteen days ago, with a request for aid; and on the arrival of the enemy in Bexar ten days ago, I sent an express to Col. F. which arrived at Goliad on the next day, urging him to send us reinforcements - none have arrived. I look to the colonies alone for aid; unless it arrives soon, I shall have to fight the enemy on his own terms. I will, however, do the best I can under the circumstances, and I feel confident that the determined valor and desperate courage, heretofore evidenced by my men, will not fail them in the last struggle, and although they may be sacrificed to the vengeance of a Gothic enemy, the victory will cost the enemy so dear, that it will be worse for him than a defeat. I hope your honorable body will hasten on reinforcements, ammunition, and provisions to our aid, as soon as possible. We have provisions for twenty days for the men we have; our supply of ammunition is limited. At least five hundred pounds of cannon powder, and two hundred rounds of six, nine, twelve, and eighteen pound balls - ten kegs of rifle powder, and a supply of lead, should be sent to this place without delay, under a sufficient guard.

If these things are promptly sent, and large reinforcements are hastened to this frontier, this neighborhood will be the great and decisive battle ground. The power of Santa Anna is to be met here or in the colonies; we had better meet them here, than to suffer a war of desolation to rage our settlements. A blood red banner waves from the church of Bexar, and in the camp above us, in token that the war is one of vengeance against rebels; they have declared us as such, and demanded that we should surrender at discretion or this garrison should be put to the sword. Their threats have had no influence on me or my men, but to make all fight with desperation, and that high-souled courage which characterizes the patriot, who is willing to die in defense of his country's liberty and his own honour.

The citizens of this municipality are all our enemies except those who have joined us heretofore; we have but three Mexicans now in the fort; those who have not joined us in this extremity, should be declared public enemies, and their property should aid in paying the expenses of the war.

The bearer of this will give you your honorable body, a statement more in detail, should he escape through the enemy's lines. God and Texas ! - Victory or Death ! !

P.S. The enemy's troops are still arriving, and the reinforcements will probably amount to two or three thousand.

A Translation of a Mexican Eyewitness Account of the Battle of the Alamo March 6, 1836
Jose Juan Sanchez-Navarro Diary Entry

"Long live our country, the Alamo is ours!

Today at five in the morning, the assault was made by four columns under the command of General Cos and Colonels Duque, Romero, and Morales. His Excellency, the President, commanded the reserves. The firing lasted half an hour. Our jefes, officers, and troops, at the same time as if by magic, reached the top of the wall, jumped within, and continued fighting with side arms. By six-thirty there was not any enemy left. I saw actions of heroic valor I envied. I was horrified by some cruelties, among others, the death of an old man named Cochran and a boy about fourteen. The women and children were saved. Travis, the commandant of the Alamo died like a hero; but (Bowie), the braggart son-in-law of Beramendi (died) like a coward. The troops were permitted to pillage. The enemy have suffered a heavy loss; twenty-one field pieces of different caliber, many arms and munitions. Two hundred fifty seven of their men were killed; I have seen and counted their bodies. But I cannot be glad because we lost eleven officers with nineteen wounded, including the valiant Duque and Gonzales; and two hundred forty-seven of our troops were wounded and one hundred ten killed. It can be truly said that with another such victory as this we'll go to the devil."

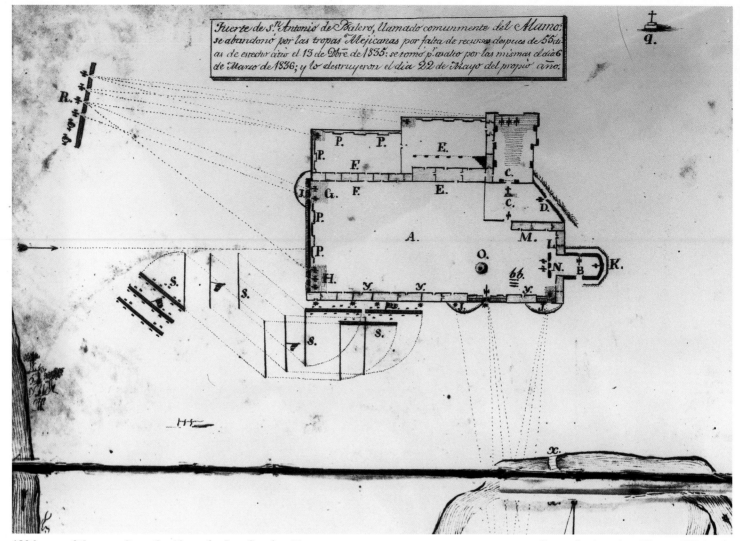

1836 map of the assault on the Alamo by Jose Sanchez-Navarro.   Center for American History, UT Austin

(Note: These two maps incorrectly show the church moved west, in line with the Convento, and the cemetery is placed out in the Plaza) Fort of San Antonio de Valero, commonly called The Alamo; abandoned by the Mexican troops without recourse after 55 days of close siege on December 13, 1835; was taken by assault in the same year on the 6th of March in 1836, and was destroyed 22 of May of the same year.

A. Plaza of Arms

B. Main gate; taken on the day of assault by Col. Juan Morales, and completed by Col. Jose Minon with the active Battalion of San Luis.

C. Ruined church, with cemetery, with a ramp formed in the nave to high battery of three cannons, called Little Fort Cos.

D. This is the weakest part of the fort. It is defined only by a stockade and a bad tree fall; from this port, in vain, when all was lost some colonists attempted to escape.

E. High barracks with corridor and corral, with its construction and the nearby church, formed the "Caballero Alto" (High Horseman, the tallest part of the fort).

F. Barracks for the troops. Col. Jose Maria Romero with the Battalions "Jimenez" and "Matamoros" assaulted and entered.

G. Battery of two cannons in its assault, where Col. Dugue was wounded. Gen. Castrillon continued the assault and entered the fort with the battalions of 500 men of Toluca and Zapadores. On the ramp of this batten, Travis, Chief of the Colonists, died like a soldier.

H. This point was intended for assault by Gen. Martin P. Cos, with a column made up of the Cazadores, Fusileros of Alameda, and Active of San Luis, but having lost many men, Cos elected an oblique movement made to the right and entered the plaza.

I. (Y) Living quarters provided with loopholes.

J. Circular trenches with ditches and stakes (stockade).

K. Ditch that defended the main gate.

L. Hospital - James Bowie died here.

M. Kitchens

N. "Espaldon" (entrenchment or barrier to defend one from an attack, a barrier of fagots, baskets, bags, etc. to guard the artillery; a half-bulwark, generally of one face and one flank).

O. Well for providing water.

P. Interior ditches and banquettes (walkway behind a parapet).

Q. Site at which 250 bodies of the colonists were burnt.

R. Battery, under construction on the night of March 4 and finished on the 5th. At this site, the reserve column, made up of the battalion of Zapadores and the Grenade Company of the other battalions at the orders of Gen Santa Anna.

S. Beginning position of the first column of Gen. Cos and direction of its march for the assault.

T. San Antonio River

V. Battery established in Bejar on the 1st of March.

X. Wood Bridge.

BB. Three cannons of iron, dismounted, were encountered in the interior of El Alamo.

50

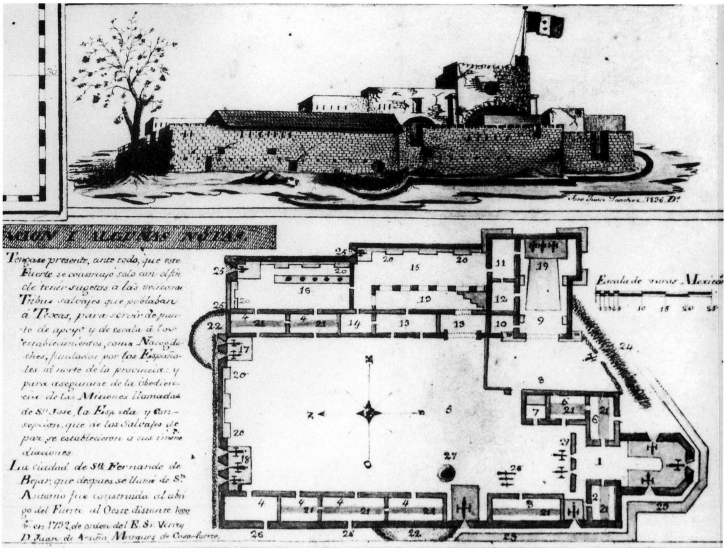

The text within the map image reads (in Spanish script):

Tengase presente, ante todo, que este
Fuerte se construyó solo con el fin
de tener sugetas a las misiones
Tribus salvajes que poblaban
á Texas, para servir de pun-
to de apoyo y de escala á los
establecimientos, como Nacog-
ches, fundados por los Españo-
les al norte de la provincia: y
para asegurarse de la obedien-
cia de las Misiones llamadas
de S.ª Jose, La España y Con-
sepción, que de los salvajes de
paz se establecieron a sus inme-
diaciones.
La ciudad de S.ª Fernando de
Bejar que despues se llamó de S.ª
Antonio fue construida al abri-
go del Fuerte al Oeste distante 1000
... en 1732 de orden del E. S.r Verrey
D. Juan de Acuña Marquis de Casa-fuerte,

1836 map and view of the Alamo by Jose Sanchez-Navarro.   Benson Latin American Library, UT Austin.

This is a detail on a 1840 map of "Estado De Parras" for Col. Jose Juan Sanchez Estrada. Above, the drawing of the Alamo is the only known image of the fort at the time of the Battle of 1836.

INDEX:

1. Main Gate.
2. Officer Guard's Room.
3. Hardware Storage.
4. Officer's Family Quarters.
5. Main Patio.
6. Hospital.
7. Kitchen.
8. Cemetery.
9. Church.
10. Gunpowder magazine.
11. Food storerooms.
12. Food storerooms.
13. Barracks.
14. Jail.
15. Horse pens.
16. Corrals and latrines.
17. Battery called Teran.
18. Battery called Condella.
19. Ramp of the Battery that they couldn't finish.
20. Interior ditch and parapet walk.
21. Trenches made by defenders.
22. Semicircular earthworks with stakes.
23. Trench started by defenders.
24. At this point, some colonist attempted to escape.
25. Points of attack and entry by Col. Duque and Romeo, ordered by Gen. Amador, with more than 500 men from Zapadores and Toluca.

Detail of 1836 map of the Alamo by Col. Ygnacio de LaBastida.
Center for American History, UT Austin

Plan of the city of San Antonio de Bexar and the fortification of the Alamo, made by Col. LaBastida, Commander of the Engineers of the Army of the North, under the direction of Gen. Filisola, Chief of the Army.

Explanation of the parts of the fort:

a.	Entrance
b.	Quarters of the officers
c.	Officer of the Guard
d.	Artillery command
e.	Artillery barracks
f.	Barracks
g.	Artillery park
h.	Interior ditch
i.	(Y) High horsemen (tallest part of the fort)
j.	Battery barbette (firing over the wall)
l.	Battery
m.	Battery
n.	Battery barbette
o.	Exterior ditch

———————————

Note: Above the Alamo are two ponds of water and a Mexican artillery position, shown in the upper right corner. A large tree is shown outside left corner of the Alamo; this is the same large old pecan tree in Jameson map and was in backyard of Maverick Home. The Alamo is shown much larger in relationship to the town across the river.

La Bastida's map clearly differs in detail from the previous two maps by Sanchez-Navarro. The contradictions in maps of this period make it difficult to accurately reconstruct the Alamo at the time of the 1836 battle.

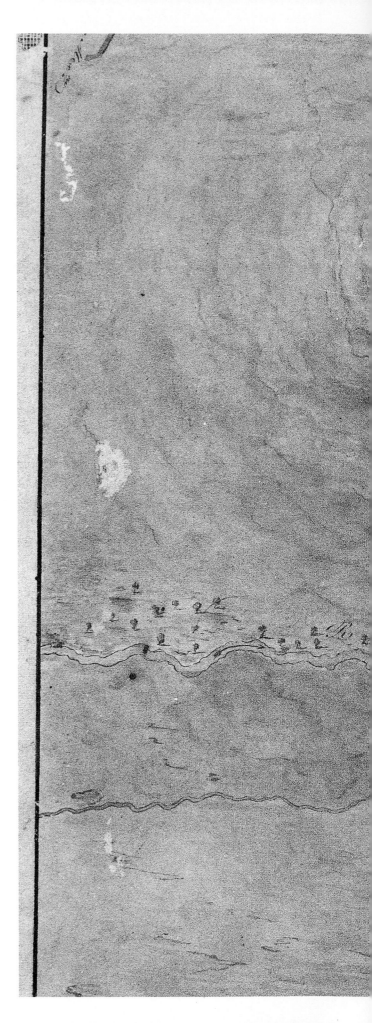

Alamo.

Villita.

Besar.

Campo Sante.

The Alameda, 1857, by Herman Lungkwitz. This double line of cottonwood trees was planted ca. 1804, about the same time the Parras (Alamo) Company moved into the Mission Valero. Alamo means cottonwood and some historians suggest these trees gave the Alamo its name. During the siege of the Alamo, the Mexican Army had an artillery emplacement and entrenchments in this area. After the Battle of the Alamo, the bodies of the defenders were burned in two funeral pyres. One pyre was located near the carts in this picture and was ten feet wide and sixty feet long. The other pyre was across the street and was about 10 feet wide and eighty feet long. The Mexican soldiers killed in the battle were buried in the town cemetery and some were thrown into the San Antonio River.

Courtesy of the San Antonio Public Library

The Mexican Army Refortifies the Alamo After the Battle

Following the Battle of the Alamo, March 6, 1836, Gen. Lopez Santa Anna marched off to the east with most of the Mexican Army. He left General Andrade with 1,001 men to garrison the town and refortify the Alamo as a strong point. The Alamo had been badly damaged from the siege and most of the buildings were in ruins; apparently, during the battle some of the rooms caught on fire also. Andrade put his men to work cleaning up the battle litter and set about fortifying the Alamo. It would be fascinating to know just what 1,000 men (some were wounded) working over 65 days did in the way of trenches, ramparts, and improved cannon positions. Unfortunately, we have no details or maps from this episode. After Santa Anna's defeat at San Jacinto on April 21, Gen. Andrade received orders dated May 19, 1836, to spike the cannons and throw the ammunition in the river, destroy all small arms, and demolish the fortifications at the Alamo. Unlike Bowie and Travis who disobeyed Gen. Houston's order to do the same thing, Andrade obeyed this order.

Andrade wrote that the Mexican soldiers left in San Antonio were down to one meal a day, the wounded had no medicines, over 200 horses had died from lack of food, men were barefoot, and the uniforms were rotting rags.

General Andrade had his soldiers make beds for those eight

Mexican soldiers too wounded to travel with the retreating army that left Bexar on May 24. Lt. Francisco Castanada and eighteen soldiers of the old Alamo Company were left behind to look after the wounded and garrison the town until the victorious Republic of Texas forces arrived. Gen. Andrade received an order not to evacuate Bexar on June 13 from Mexico City, but by that time he was already a five days march away.

Dr. J. H. Barnard, who had been a prisoner of war, noted in his journal: "Sunday, May 22, 1836, General Adrade has received orders to destroy the Alamo and proceed to join the main army at Goliad. The troops have hitherto been busy in fortifying the Alamo. They are now as busy as bees, tearing down the walls, etc...

Tuesday, May 24, 1836 (6:00 P.M.) As the troops left town this morning, a large fire streamed up from the Alamo. ... We found the fire proceeding from a church where a platform had been built extending from the great door to the top wall on the back side. ...This was made of wood and was too far consumed ... to extinguish it. ...The Alamo was completely dismantled, all single walls were leveled, the fosse filled up, and the pickets torn up and burnt."

Apparently a Mexican warship (Brigantine) was named "The Vanquisher of the Alamo" in honor of the battle of the Alamo and sent from Veracruz to Texas on April 28, 1836.

The Alamo during the Republic of Texas 1836 - 1845

1836-45 - The Republic of Texas Period

The transfer of the Alamo and San Antonio, from Lt. Francisco Castañada and his eighteen Alamo Company soldiers to Col. Juan Seguin and his twenty or so men, went peacefully. Seguin claimed when he arrived in the spring of 1836, only about forty families remained in San Antonio. Most of these chose to follow Lt. Castañeda, leaving perhaps fifty persons in town.

After two sieges and two battles, many houses were burnt, battered by cannon fire, or looted. Fences were torn up, fields and orchards destroyed, and cattle and horses scattered or stolen. Soon, 200 Anglo-American volunteers under Col. James Smith arrived.

Ashes of the Defenders Interred

Col. Seguin claimed to have gathered up the ashes, burnt bone fragments of the Alamo defenders and performed a military funeral service before placing them in San Fernando Church. However, Dr. John Sutherland claims that in early February, 1837, while Capt. Lockart and his rangers were passing through San Antonio, they gathered the ashes, placed them in a large coffin, and buried it, with military honors in a peach orchard near the Alamo. A third version of the burial appeared in Mr. J.M. Rodriguez's memoirs, and claimed that Alcalde Francisco Ruiz ordered the remains collected and given a proper burial. Just where, was not stated.

June 20, 1836 - Col. Juan Seguin was ordered to command the people of Bexar to drive in all the cattle to town to "demonstrate their loyalty" to the new government. Any who didn't comply would be treated as an enemy of Texas. All Republic of Texas troops retreated to Victoria because rumor had it that the Mexican Army was returning. This proved to be a false alarm.

October 17, 1836 - Col. Juan Seguin returned to occupy San Antonio with seventy or eighty men on foot. They were recruited from Gen. Rusk's camp near Victoria and found horses to become cavalry around San Antonio. They were under orders to watch out for Mexican military movements, arrest suspicious persons, avoid clashes with Comanches, and round up mules, horses, and cattle where ever they find them. This last order would lead to wholesale rustling of livestock by Anglo-American soldiers from San Antonio de Bexar down the San Antonio River to Goliad. This order was officially rescinded in 1837, but the practices went unpunished for decades. Col. Seguin attempted to maintain good relations with the new Anglo-American government as well as rally support for it with the native Mexican Texans. This would soon prove very difficult.

December 1836 - Col. Seguin reported 80 American Republic of Texas troops and about 200 Mexican "Civil Militia"; apparently, some Mexican families had returned. However, most of the local Mexicans remained lukewarm to the new regime. Most of the Republic of Texas troopers were recruited from East Texas around Houston and Galveston from recent arrivals from the U.S.

January 1837 - Claiming the Mexican Army was soon to return to San Antonio, Gen. Felix Huston, commander of the Republic of Texas Army, ordered Col. Seguin to evacuate the town and destroy it totally , thereby avoiding a second battle of the Alamo. It was rumored that this was a dark scheme to remove the native Mexican settlers and grab their homes and land on the part of Gen. Felix

Huston and Lt. Col. Alonso Sweitzer. Col. Seguin complained and President Houston told him to use his judgement. San Antonio was not destroyed. Seguin left 10 men guarding the town and withdrew.

Occupation of the Alamo by Republic of Texas Troops

January 1, 1839 - Two companies of Republic of Texas Cavalry, under Captain George Howard, entered San Antonio and occupied the "Alamo Barracks." This is the first firm mention of reoccupation of the ruined fort following the battle. Col. Lysander Wells arrived and perhaps then drew the early sketch of the Alamo. These cavalry troops left to join Col. Edward Burleson in driving the Cherokee out of Texas. Only a handful of Republic of Texas soldiers were left to guard military supplies stored at the Alamo.

August 20, 1839 - Samuel Maverick, former member of the Alamo garrison and now head of the city council in Bexar, wrote Captain Miguel Arciniega of the Civil Militia to take steps to defend the Alamo and La Villita neighborhoods from Indian or bandit attacks. All the men should be ready for action and six or more men were to stand guard each night.

April 2, 1840 - "Mayor Smith informed the Council that the Rev. Mr. Valdez desires to buy some of the stone lying(sic) at the walls of the Alamo. The Corporation resolved to sell him all the stone he may want at fifty cents per car load. Approved." Whether the stones were to be used at San Fernando Cathedral, which was in a sad state of disrepair and at which Father Jose Antonio Valdez served at the time, is not known. Four months later, Father John Mary Odin, Vice-Prefect Apostolic of Texas, withdrew Valdez's "Faculties" (along with those of the aged Father Garza) for living in open concubinage and other derelictions of duty.

December, 1840 - A company of Republic of Texas troops returned to occupy the Alamo once again.

March 5, 1841 - Gen. Rafael Vasquez entered San Antonio de Bexar and reoccupied the town and the Alamo in the name of the Republic of Mexico. With him was a force of 700, made up of regular Mexican troops, 30 Caddo Indians, and a volunteer cavalry unit of local San Antonio Mexican men from San Antonio. Little is known about what they did during the stay in town, but there may have been some sort of memorial at the Alamo. Most Anglos retreated at the approach of the Mexicans, except for three Anglo men who remained sitting on the walls of the Alamo. They were unmolested by the Mexicans. After a few days, the Mexican Army withdrew.

May, 1841 - A mutiny at the Alamo occurred with the Republic of Texas troops. Two mutineers were shot and order was restored.

September 10, 1842 - Mexican Army reoccupies San Antonio

Gen. Adrian Woll encircled the town of San Antonio with a force made up again of Mexican soldiers, Cherokee Indians under Vicente Cordova, and a volunteer unit of local San Antonio Mexicans. The 54 men called themselves "Defendores de Bexar." They were lead by Juan Seguin, who by this time had turned against the Republic. Seguin and his men were placed in the Alamo and the Indians guarded the street leading there.

At dawn, the Mexicans entered downtown Bexar to the music of the dance tune "La Cachucha". Samuel Maverick was captured. Gen. Woll appointed new city officers and stayed a few days. He fired a cannon to celebrate the 16th of September and held a dance in honor of the ladies of the town. It was said to be well attended.

Capt. Hays goes to the Alamo and picks a fight

Capt. Jack Hays, with a ten of men, rode up to the Alamo from the east and taunted the Mexicans to come out and fight in hopes of leading them into an ambush. He apparently thought only about 50 would come out. Instead, a very large force of Mexicans rode out of the Alamo and chased Hays all the way to the Salado Creek, at which time the Battle of Salado Creek took place. The Mexican Army later retreated to the Rio Grande with a large number of local Mexican families.

September 25, 1842 - A large force of Anglos entered the town and held a meeting of about 1,200 persons in front of the Alamo. Vice President Burleson stood in a window of the Alamo and made a speech in favor of an invasion of Mexico. Another speaker stated that "their intention was to capture and kill the last Mexican on this continent."

Vandalism at the Alamo

Over the next two months, while a force was being raised, the Anglo men explored the Alamo, carved their names in the walls, and broke pieces off the walls for souvenirs. Bill Bates was said to have cut the heads off of two figures representing angels on each side of the Alamo door. Two large wooden statues were said to be laying prostrate in front of the Alamo. Harvey Adams cut a piece of wood from one and made a large pipe out of it, carving "the whole Alamo" on the pipe.

The statues were probably those of St. Francis and St. Dominic that stood in the niches on either side of church doors and described in the inventories of 1772 and 1793. Other mission statues were vandalized and used for target practice including those at Mission San Jose.

Samuel Maverick and the Alamo

Samuel Maverick, was, one of the most influential individuals who impacted the evolution of Alamo Plaza. He arrived in San Antonio from South Carolina just before the start of the siege of Bexar in 1835, to engage in land speculation. He acted as a spy during the siege and made a map to aide the rebel's capture of the town. Elected as representative to the Convention of 1836, for the defenders of the Alamo, he missed being killed in the battle. He had a strong attachment to the Alamo, and wished to live within sight of where his friends had died. By his subdividing the land, the old compound surrounded by open fields became engulfed by urban sprawl and he demolished most, if not all, of the old remaining houses along the west wall. He had moved his family to San Antonio in 1838, and started acquiring land around Alamo Plaza in 1841. He moved his family into one of the old Indian quarters while he built a two-story home in the northwest corner of the old mission compound. In 1848, he subdivided all the land west, north and northeast of the old mission and called the project "Alamo City." During foundation excavations on the Maverick property, old Alamo cannons were found that were buried by the Mexican Army at the end of May, 1836.

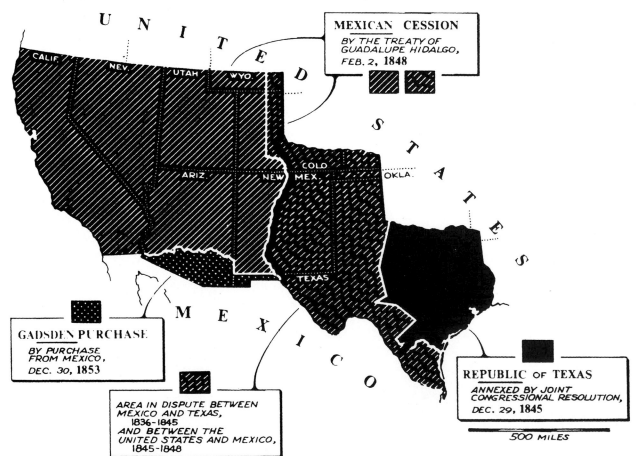

MEXICAN TERRITORY
ACQUIRED BY
THE UNITED STATES, 1845-1853

MEXICAN CESSION
BY THE TREATY OF
GUADALUPE HIDALGO,
FEB. 2, **1848**

GADSDEN PURCHASE
BY PURCHASE
FROM MEXICO,
DEC. 30, **1853**

AREA IN DISPUTE BETWEEN
MEXICO AND TEXAS,
1836-1845
AND BETWEEN THE
UNITED STATES AND MEXICO,
1845-1848

REPUBLIC OF TEXAS
ANNEXED BY JOINT
CONGRESSIONAL RESOLUTION,
DEC. 29, **1845**

500 MILES

First Proposed Monument To Honor Dead Mexican Soldiers By Jose Juan Sanchez-Navarro 1836

"After the capture of the Alamo, I proposed to the commandant General, Don Martin Perfecto de Cos, that the valiant officers and soldiers who died in the assault be buried in the cemetery of the chapel of the said fort, that the names of each be inscribed on a copper tablet made from one of the cannons captured to be placed on a column at the base of which these eight lines might be written:

Second Proposed Monument To Honor Alamo Defenders 1840-1842

Alamo Stones carved into souvenirs

During 1840 and 1842, sculptor William Nangle was carving Alamo stones into miniature monuments, urns, candle sticks, vases, and pipes. He made a six-foot high monument he hoped the Texas government would buy. The monument (below) was placed at the State Capital where it was damaged in a fire.

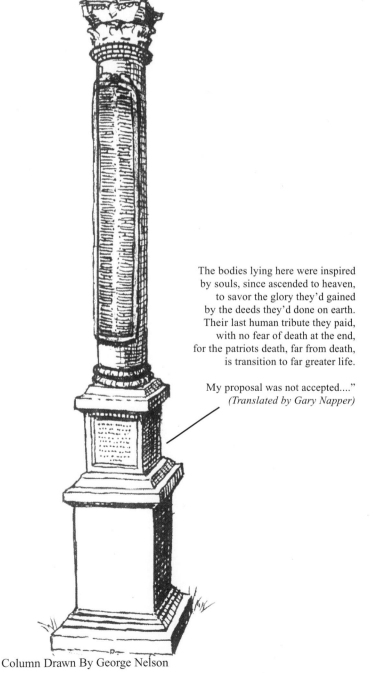

The bodies lying here were inspired
by souls, since ascended to heaven,
to savor the glory they'd gained
by the deeds they'd done on earth.
Their last human tribute they paid,
with no fear of death at the end,
for the patriots death, far from death,
is transition to far greater life.

My proposal was not accepted...."
(Translated by Gary Napper)

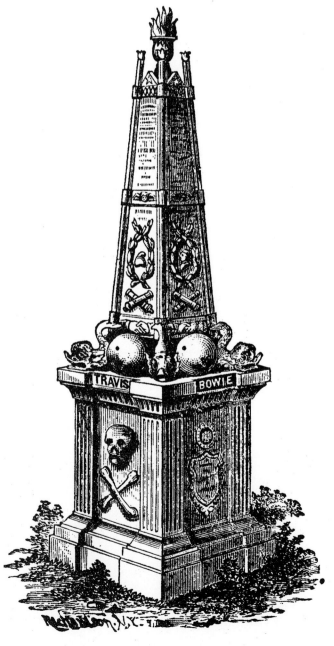

Column Drawn By George Nelson

Sam Maverick's Subdivision "Alamo City"

These two maps record Sam Maverick's real estate plans for the land around the Alamo. The map to the right shows the old Spanish land grants around the Alamo and his plans for street and lots are faintly superimposed. Each old land grant has the chain of title from the Spanish government down to Maverick's purchase. The old Spanish land grants were wedged shaped to take advantage of natural drainage from irrigation ditches.

The map below dates from 1849 and carefully shows the surveyor notes for the old Alamo walls. Archaeologists found that this map is highly accurate in showing the old outline of the Alamo walls.

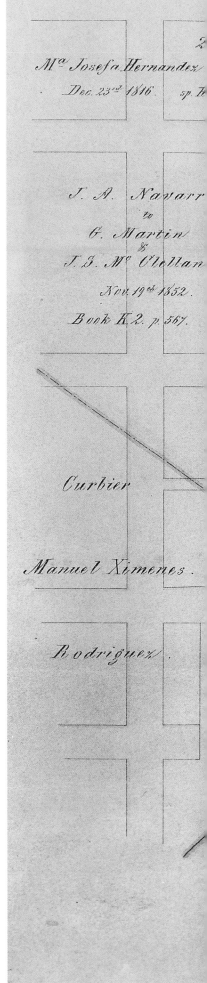

Map of the Alamo in 1849, by Francois Giraud, the City Surveyor (City Engineers Office Book 1, page 114).

Juan Frco Collantes.

k 2. p. 357 & 358.

Suerte No 24.

Sp. Govt to Miguel Losoya Febr. 25th 1793.

do to Capt Frco Garcia Nov 23rd 1819.

sp. Rec. Book 3. p 156 & 157.

Candelaria de la Garza to S. A. Maverick Sep. 10th 1851.

Book K.1. p. 261.

Suerte No 25.

Sp. Govt to Cipriano Losoya Febr. 25th 1793.

Manuel Losoya, son, to Vicente Cortari Jun 10th 1820. sp. Rec. Vol. 3.
pp 19, 20 & 21.

Vicente Cortari by will to M. Estrada June 23rd 1834. Prob. Rec.
Book A. pp 113-114.

Heirs of Estrada to S. A. Maverick part north of red line
in 4 deeds.

viz 1st Apr 12th 1844. C.2. p 132. 2nd Dec 6th 1847 G.1. p 443.

3rd July 20th 1848 G.1. p. 443. 4th Oct 30th 1849.
H.1. p. 431.

Widow of
Vicente Amador

Juana de los Santos

Superviele & Marshal

present Ditch
old Ditch

Susan Francis McKay Ximenez Costanho
y Soto
to S. A. Maverick
Apr 19 1841 K.1. p. 445

Mariano Roman
to
S. A. Maverick.
July 27th 1841. A.2. p 470.

Alamo
Plaza.

ACEQUIA MADRE

Antonio River.

Concepcion Charte.

Partition Oct 30th 1849.

Plaza
de
Valero.

G. Freislehen

The Alamo ca. 1839, attributed to Lysander Well. Note: low cemetery wall in front of church.   University of the Incarnate Word.

The Alamo ca. 1839, The Alamo ruins with Texas Flag Flying from the roof. Drawing by William Bisset, 1839.   ITC.

Ruins of the Alamo, ca. 1839-40, from, *Map and Description of Texas,* 1840.   ITC.
Note: low stone cemetery wall in front of Church.

Early tourist pictures of the Alamo - 1839-1844

At far right is an awkward attempt to draw the Galera.   The Center for American History, UT Austin.

ca. 1844 - Distant view of the Alamo looking east, by William Bolleart.   Newberry Library.
Note: small house in front of Church. It appears to be part of the ruined west wall and may be part of the Charli property.

The U.S. Army and the Alamo - 1845-1861

The Arrival of the U.S. Army before Annexation

Almost two months before the annexation of Texas to the U.S., Col. William S. Harney arrived in San Antonio on October 28, 1845, with three companies of the 2nd U.S. Dragoons.

The U.S. Soldiers camped at San Pedro Springs, northwest of town, at the old city park where the Spanish Army first established the presidio (fort) in 1718. Surely they visited the Alamo. Brigadier General John E. Wool, commander of the Army of the Center, began gathering men and supplies in San Antonio for an invasion of Mexico. When some of the volunteer units marched off to invade Mexico, they stopped at the Alamo and dug bullets out of the walls for souvenirs.

One young volunteer, Edward Everett, an artist, was shot in the knee by a drunken Anglo-Texan and could not march with the invasion force. Everett was quite talented and left some of the best images and maps of the Alamo.

Edward Everett's Memoirs of Repairing the Alamo

"Early in the spring of 1847, the idea of turning the then ruinous Alamo building to some account as a depot for army stores, and for offices, workshops, etc., was entertained. These buildings having been used by Texas as a fortification in their war with Mexico, they became by the treaty of annexation the property of the United States. Captain Ralston, seeing that they could be made available at an inconsiderable expense, and having obtained permission from the quartermaster general, proceeded to put the plan in execution, and by his direction, I made out plans and estimates for placing them in serviceable condition, in which my knowledge of construction became available. In the course of a few months, these ruins were converted into ample storehouses for quartermaster property, and others for ordnance property and medicine stores, forage houses, blacksmiths, carpenters, wagon makers, harness and other workshops, also stabling and mule yards. Besides these, a convenient office and quarters for Captain Ralston, and myself and other clerks were fitted up.

The lumber for the roofs, floors, etc., of Southern pine, shingles, etc., was obtained from Bastrop, and hauled from there a distance of about one hundred miles, timber suitable for the purpose not being obtainable nearer. The ruinous portions of the walls were repaired, and the old plaster or concrete roofs removed, in which operations many thousand of bats were unceremoniously evicted, and rendered homeless, and from that time each was dependent for a lodging literally on his own hook.

The buildings thus remodeled, extended (see plan) from the corner next to the church, along the east line of the quadrangle, a length of about two hundred feet. They averaged about eighteen to twenty feet wide outside and twelve to eighteen inside. The height of the walls was twenty feet and over, so that in parts we put in floors midway. The office was in the south end, and Captain Ralston had a room 'round the corner. They were fitted up with rough tables, stools and cot bedsteads. These quarters being elevated one story above the ground, and having plastered walls, glass windows and a wooden floor, were a vast improvement on those we before occupied.

I can present nothing new regarding the history of the Alamo, but can only give the account of the condition in which we found it in 1846-47, and subsequent developments on clearing away the debris of the fallen walls and roofs. There was no pretensions to ornamental architecture except in the facade of the church, and portions of its interior. Such of the other buildings as remained, having the usual thick and roughly-built stone walls, and heavy plaster roofs. These we rebuilt and adapted to our purposes without remorse, but the church we respected as an historical relic - and as such its characteristics were not marred by us. We had the debris cleared away from the interior, in which process several skeletons and other relics of the siege were found. I regret to see by a later engraving of this ruin, that tasteless hands have evened off the rough walls, as they were left after the siege, surmounting them with a ridiculous scroll, giving the building the appearance of the headboard of a bedstead. The care thus shown, however questionable the taste of its execution, is highly commendable, when compared with the wanton destruction with which other curious buildings in the vicinity have been visited, by relic hunters, or other vandals and iconoclasts.

The keystone over the front entrance bore the date, 1758. Numerous shot holes and the demolished roof and probably towers, bore testimony to the severity of the bombardment; this part, from its stronger walls, having been restored to as the last stronghold of the devoted band. On either side of the entrance was a small vaulted room, having each a small window opening to the front. The roof had been of stone, of a semicircular arch springing from the side walls, which were as usual in the form of the Latin cross, and were well and solidly built. Adjoining the transept on one side was a vaulted room strongly built of stone, which we made use of, after properly securing the entrances, as a magazine, in which was stored the large amount of ammunition in our hands."

Masonic Lodge at the Alamo

In the late 1840's when Mr. Edward was the Alamo, his commanding officer, Captain Ralston, allowed a Masonic Lodge to be established upstairs in the old convento (long barracks). Apparently quite a few Alamo defenders, including Bowie, Travis, Crockett, and other defenders were members of the York Masonic Lodge. Santa Ana and other Mexican leaders were members of the Scottish Rite Masonic lodge. A Plaque commemorating these Masons is on the old convento wall.

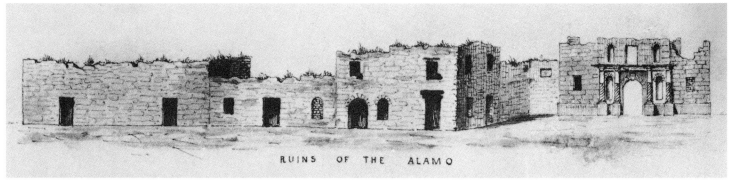

ca. 1845, Drawing by Lt. Edward Blake Courtesy of the National Archives.

Drawing by Edward Everett showing his repairs to the old Convento, ca. 1847. Courtesy of the National Archives.

Montage combining the above drawing of the Convento with an 1860's photograph of US Army quartermaster wagons at the Alamo Church. The church has a new facade and roof built, ca. 1850. Note: chimney appears above the Convento at the left.   ITC.

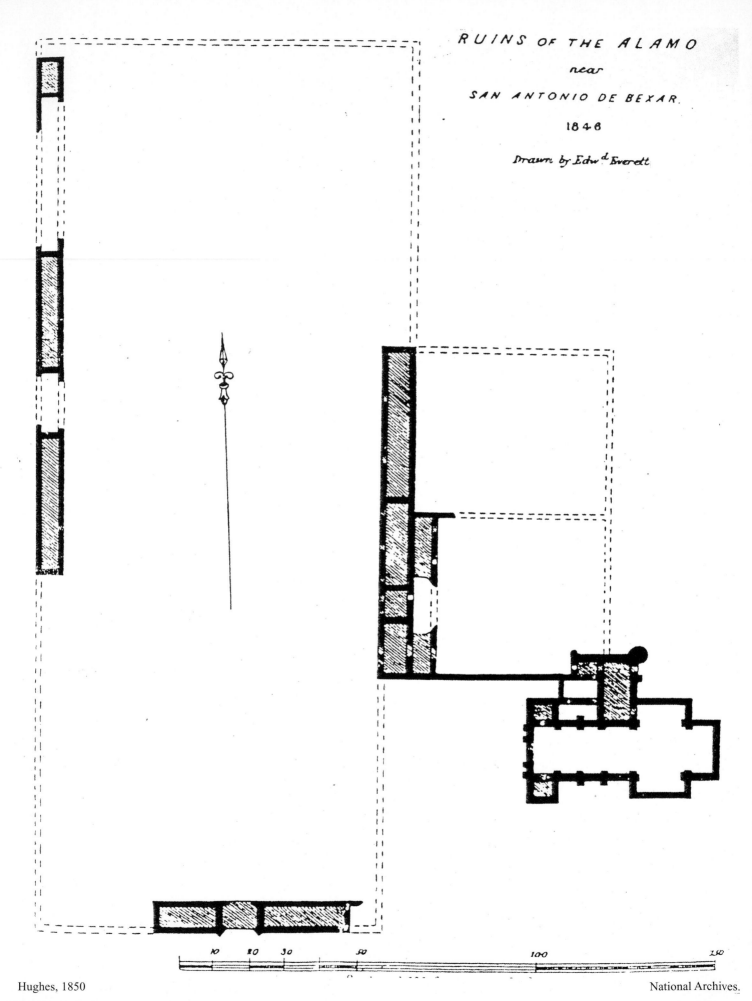

RUINS OF THE ALAMO
near
SAN ANTONIO DE BEXAR.
1846

Drawn by Edw.d Everett

Hughes, 1850

National Archives.

64

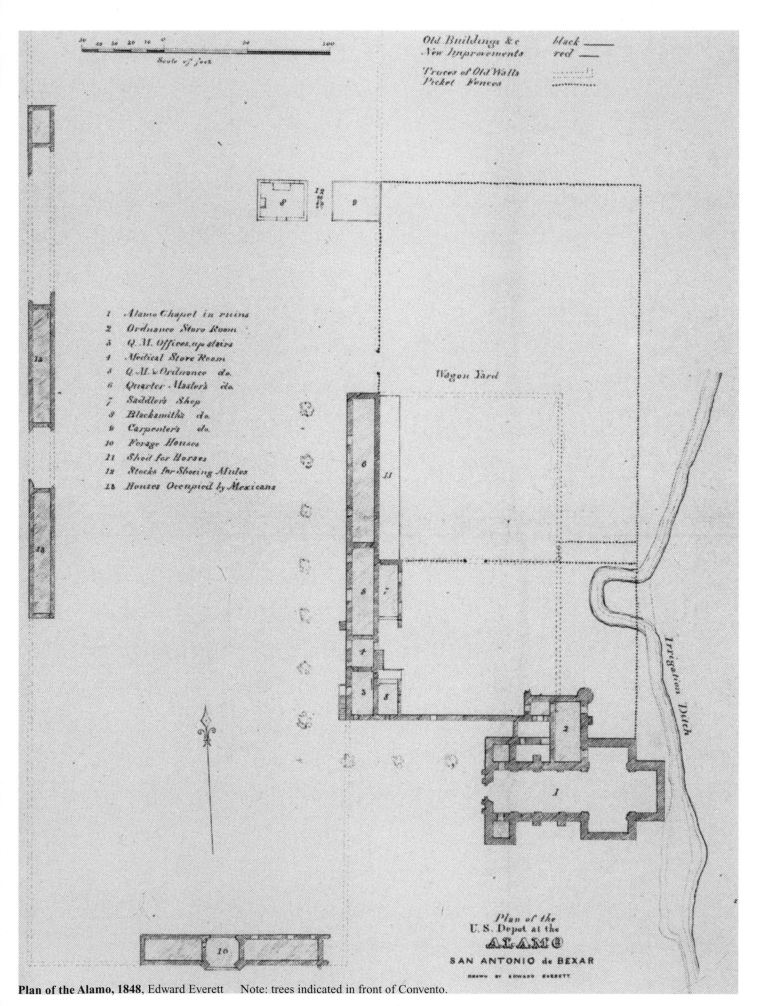

Plan of the Alamo, 1848, Edward Everett   Note: trees indicated in front of Convento.

1849 U.S. Army Map of the Alamo

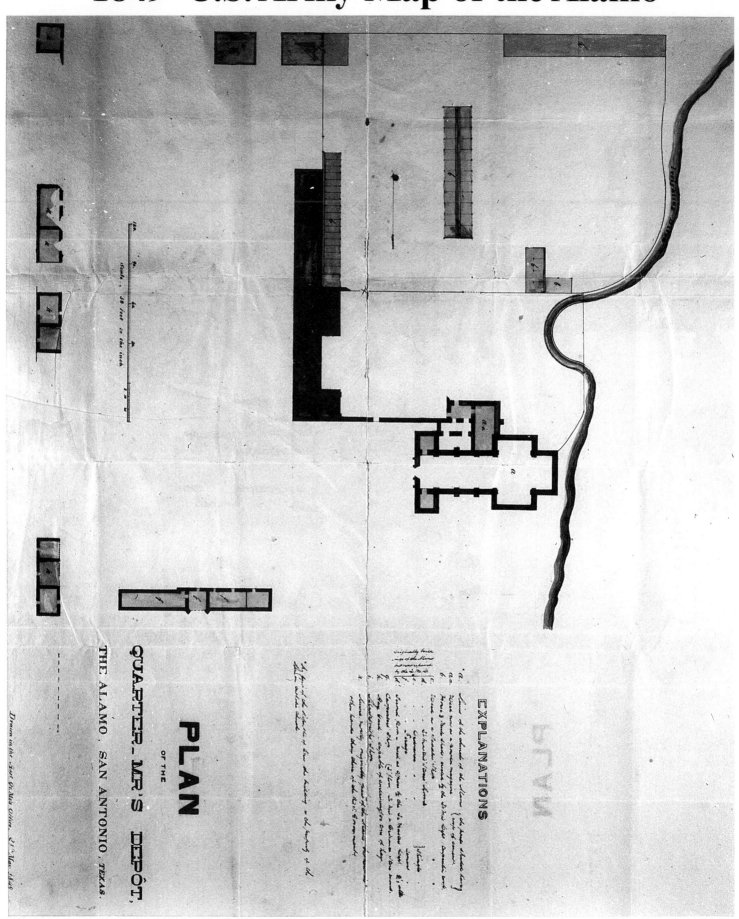

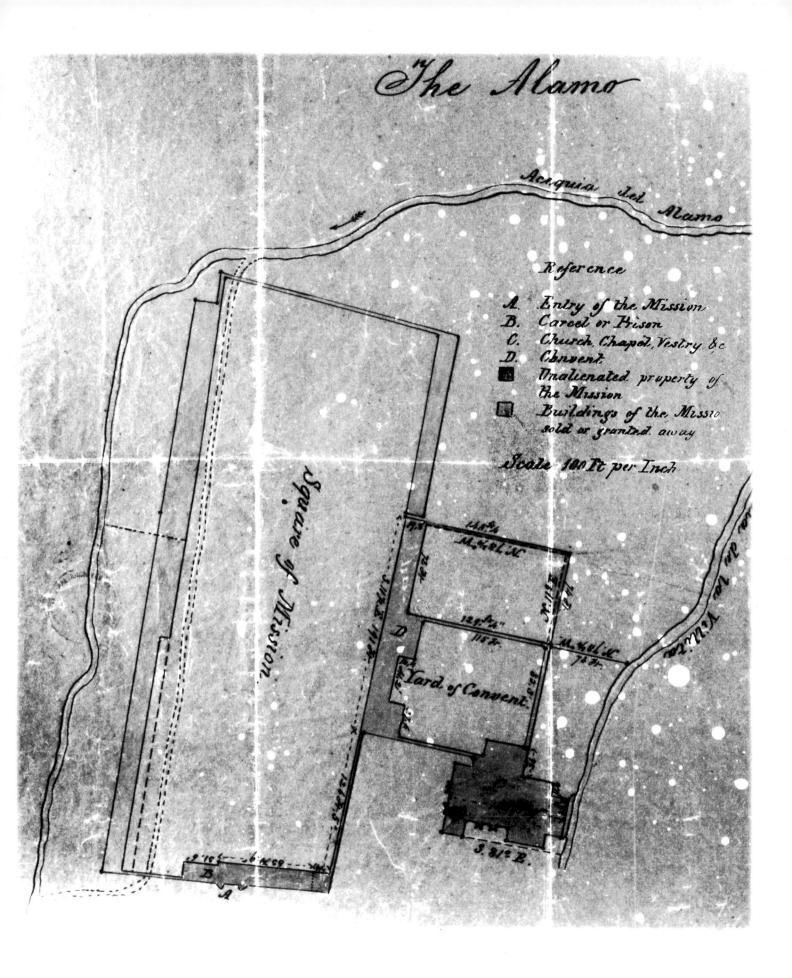

ca. 1849, **Map of the Alamo,** similar to Giraud map on pp.57. (Map not actual size of original. 1 inch does not equal100 feet exactly) National Archives.

Daguerreotype of the Alamo, 1849. First known photo.　　　　Gift of Gov. Dolph Briscoe, Center for American History, UT Austin.

The Alamo by Theodore Gentiliz. Note: carved stone plaques in top of wall at left. Holes shown in stone walls are remains of scaffolding during construction of the Church in the 1700s.

DRT Library.

Two Drawings Made from the Exact Same Point of View 1847-48

The Alamo, 1848, Capt. Seth Eastman.   Peabody Museum, Harvard University.

Ruins of the church of the Alamo, 1847, Edward Everett. Note: apparent battle damage.   Amon Carter Museum.

Rear of Alamo Church, 1848, by Capt. Arthur T. Lee. Note: marshy area behind church; in center left is the end of the Galera, beyond, is the Charli house.   Rochester Historical Society.

Rear of Alamo, by Theodore Gentilz.   Note: scaffold holes in church walls.   Courtesy of Witte Museum.

Rear of Alamo, 1849, Capt. Seth Eastman. Note: pond behind church. Figures on top of wall are near point of view in following pages.

Witte Museum.

Rear of Alamo with new wooden roof and facade; detail of painting by Herman Lungkwitz, 1857. Note: new windows and rear portions have been lowered, and a strange feature on right edge of picture.

Original at Witte Museum, photo from DRT Library.

Drawings and Photograph Provide a

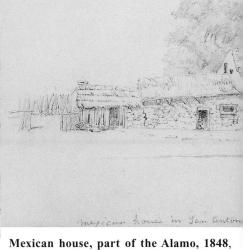

View west over the top of the Alamo Church, 1844, William Bolleart. House in center is at site of the Charli house. Picket fence in location of old west wall. Small square in foreground is the window of the church. San Fernando Church in background. Courtesy of the Newberry Library.

Mexican house, part of the Alamo, 1848, Capt. Seth Eastman. The rebuilt Trevino house with gabled roof, to the right are two arches of an old ruined mission Indian quarters.

McNay Art Museum.

Interior view of Alamo Church, 1847, by Edward Everett, Amon Carter Museum
View west, San Fernando Church in background. Similar view to above. (compare to page 97)

Panorama of the West Side of Alamo Plaza.

The Maverick Home ca. 1850-60, looking northwest at the corner of Houston Street and Avenue D on Alamo Plaza, built at the northwest corner of the old Alamo compound. The large pecan tree survived the Battle of the Alamo.   Grand Jean collection, DRT.

View from Alamo, ca. 1849, South toward Plaza de Valero, Low Barracks at right. By Seth Eastman   Peabody Museum, Harvard.

Mission San Jose ca. 1847, by Edward Everett. Note: bell-shaped ornament with niche over arches. Also, the house with three arches above the cart is very similar to the old Indian quarters along the west wall of the Alamo. Amon Carter Museum.

Mission Chapel of San Jose 5 miles from San Antonio. Texas   *Nov. 24 1848*

Mission San Jose, 1848, Capt. Seth Eastman. Bell-shaped ornament shown here disappears in pictures of San Jose more often after this date.

Did the Bell Shaped Facade of the Alamo come from Mission San Jose?

Mid-nineteenth century engraving by Louderback Hoffman (After Emory). Note: ornament above arches. From drawings by Eastman and Everett, an ornament (with a niche) once stood over the arches behind San Jose Mission in 1846-48, but disappeared sometime later. Was this the same stone ornament, or did the Army just get the design idea from it and someone else took it? In the past, Architect John Fries was given the credit for the design of the famous facade.

Photo of Mission San Jose ca. 1900's. Note: bell shaped ornament is missing from above the arches.   Texas Parks and Wildlife Dept.

The Alamo gets its Famous Bell Shaped Parapet

**Campanulate,
bellshaped ornament**

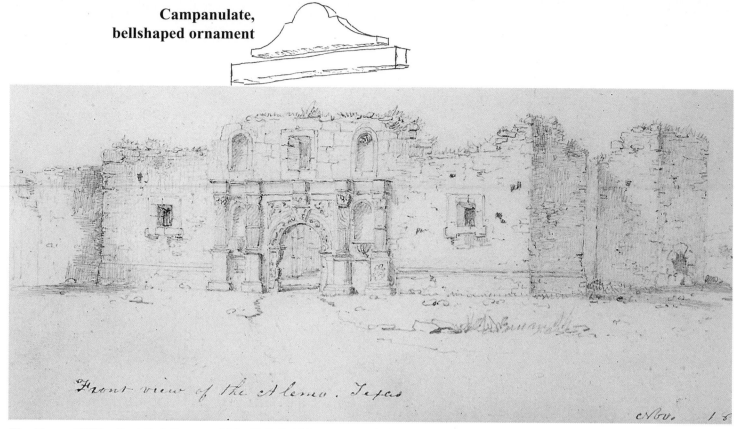

The Alamo, 1848 by Capt. Seth Eastman. Major E. B. Babbitt recommended demolishing the old stone walls and building a new warehouse, but Gen. S. Jesup ordered just the repairs of the existing church building. This decision, either for budget reasons or historical preservation, saved the old church. Major Babbit had a wooden roof put on the church and a second floor put in the nave. The famous Campanulate (bell-shaped) facade was added to close in the west gable of the new roof in 1850.   McNay.

The Alamo, 1844, by William Bolleart. From this angle, Galera (old barracks, jail and main gate) appears to join the church.   The Newberry Library.

1860's photo of Alamo Church with new bellshaped facade. Note wagon scale in foreground. **Lawsuits over ownership of the Alamo.** At the end of 1848, Edward Everett went with Capt. Ralston to Washington and Capt. M. Morris took over the Quartermaster storehouse at the Alamo. A flurry of lawsuits broke out over the Alamo, involving the U.S. Army, Bishop John M. Odin of the Catholic Church, the city of San Antonio, Samuel Maverick, and various "squatters" over the ownership and control of the Alamo grounds. Bishop Odin won ownership of the church and, for a while, considered selling the rocks in the old walls to fund a local college. In 1845, he proposed to use the rock to build a new college. The U.S. Army moved in on January 2, 1849, at which time the Catholic Church demanded, and got, $150 a month rent. Sam Maverick got $200 a month rent for his lot used by the Army. Grandjean Collection DRT Library.

The Alamo, San Antonio, Texas ca. 1860, redrawn by John James Young. Army Art Collection, courtesy Ben Huseman.   Amon Carter Museum.

The Civil War starts at the Alamo

February 16, 1861

Although the firing on Ft. Sumter, April 12, 1861, in Charleston Harbor generally marks the start of the Civil War, two months earlier a coup took place at the Alamo. This coup was carried out by a secret white supremacy group called the Knights of the Golden Circle (KGC), with the willing help of General David E. Twiggs, temporary commander of all US Troops in Texas. General Twiggs was a pro-slavery Southerner who, after surrendering all US Troops and material to the local KGC, resigned his US Commission and became a Confederate General. Robert E. Lee, at this time still a U.S. Army Colonel, was in command of all federal forces in Texas until receiving orders to proceed to Washington, D.C. Records show Lee was prepared to defend federal property and troops from attacks by secessionists, as his oath required. Twiggs, on the other hand, clearly did all he could to aid the KGC groups to seize around 2,500 federal troops and over $1,600,000 (some say $3 million), in military supplies without firing a shot.

The Knights of the Golden Circle

The Knights of the Golden Circle, formed in the mid-1850's, had secret handshakes, signs, passwords, and rituals. Its meeting places were called "Castles." The Golden Circle referred to a circle 2,000 miles across with Havana, Cuba, the center pivot. Their top secret internal papers limited membership to white men who believed in expanding slavery. Interestingly, a few Hispanics in San Antonio became associated with the movement. KGC members wrote that they thought at least half of the 8,235 citizens of San Antonio were pro-Union, along with the local militia company.

Political Meeting at Alamo Plaza Disrupted

The election of November, 1860, had been a hot one in Texas. A rally in October, 1860, was held in the south end of the Alamo Plaza in front of the Menger Hotel. A large crowd of mixed factions gathered before a platform to hear speeches by a popular Episcopal Methodist Bishop who supported secession, slavery, and states' rights, and a Mr. Anderson, for the Union. The Bishop was allowed to give a fiery secession speech, but when Mr. Anderson began his speech, the "boys" (KGC), with pistols in hand, stormed the platform and cleared the stage with pistol shots. Later, the pro-union newspaper, The Alamo <u>Express</u>, was attacked and burnt to the ground.

Two members of the Knights of the Golden Circle from the San Antonio area wrote accounts of this period - Morgan M. Merrick and R. H. Williams (an Englishman). Williams joined the night that the KGC broke up the political meeting. Stating the organization was "ostensibly formed to protect Southern rights, its real object was to bring about secession, and all its weight was thrown into that movement." Merrick wrote in his journal, "The KGC - a military organization that was powerful throughout the U.S. and whose primary object was acquisition of territory outside the boundary of the U.S." After the election of Abraham Lincoln in November, 1861, the KGC pushed for a convention in Austin. Governor Sam Houston opposed succession, although a slave owner himself. He had been a leader of the "Know-Nothing" party in the 1850's and now tried to divert the energy building toward a civil war into a new invasion of Mexico to grab more land. Governor Houston was rejected and the ordinance of secession was signed February 1, 1861.

For the next two weeks, the 2,500 federal troops in Texas were in limbo; rumors abounded of bands of armed secessionists, intending to seize US Forts and supplies.

Panorama of south end of Plaza de Valero

ITC

Secessionists seize the Alamo from the U.S. Army, February 16, 1861 - from Harpers *Weekly*. Note: old Galera to the right of the church, appears to have a second story. Church shown with caryatids (female shaped columns). ITC.

Site of political rally broken up by the Knights of the Golden Circle.
Taken from balcony of the Menger Hotel. Alamo Plaza off page to right.

The Alamo at the Time of the Civil War

Until the arrival of Col. C. A. Watts, who was to assume command at San Antonio, Gen. Twiggs remained temporarily in charge. The KGC then moved to seize the U.S. Military supplies. A group of three "Commissioners on behalf of Commission of Public Safety," Thomas J. Devine, P.N. Luckett, and Samuel A. Maverick, were appointed to demand General Twiggs surrender all troops and supplies to them.

General Twiggs

General Twiggs arms the KGC

An astounding entry in Mr. Merrick's journal of February, 1861, states that Gen. Twiggs, armed with the best rifles, was the very force that would attack his troops. Merrick wrote that General Twiggs was requested by Dr. Cupples and Judge Welder of the KGC to provide arms for one company of infantry. Twiggs granted this request but the ordinance officer, Capt. Whightly, tried to issue old obsolete Mexican War guns. When Twiggs heard of this, he ordered that new Springfield rifles be issued instead. They were turned over to Merrick who was the ordinance officer of the KGC.

Knights of the Golden Circle make their move

Feb 15, 1861 - During the night, the soldiers guarding the Alamo were ordered not to load their muskets and not to resist in case an armed force attempted to seize the public property stored there.

Samuel A. Maverick

The local KGC company of 150 went active that night, along with about 150 other local men. They were joined by about the same number from Atascosa, Medina, and other areas to the west. Col. Ben McCullough stated he led about 400 additional volunteers to San Antonio, bringing the number to about 800 to 1,000 (some sources claim 1,100). Only 160 federal troops defended the three Army depots: The Alamo, the Arsenal, and the Commissary buildings.

One of the KGC units was called the "Company of Alamo Guards," and was led by Capt. Edgar. February 16, 1860, at four o'clock in the morning, the KGC troops began surrounding all U.S. Army positions. After Gen. Twiggs surrendered all troops, forts, and military supplies in Texas, the 160 federal soldiers (some say 120), marched out of San Antonio to the beat of drums and camped at San Pedro Springs. In the afternoon at the Alamo, the safe of Capt. Reynolds was seized and between $9,000 and $10,000 was confiscated. A sergeant told his commander that the men "would resist all attempts, and die with their arms in their hands." United States soldiers, upon arriving in San Antonio, beat their rifles on the ground to break them so the traitors could not use them. The U.S. Army sergeant stationed at the Alamo went over to the Confederate side and remained at the Alamo.

After the coup, the KGC men went on a drinking spree and then went home, except for 70 local men who guarded the captured supplies which were transferred to the Alamo. Gen. Twiggs was condemned as a traitor by the Union Army. The Texas State Legislature proclaimed him a patriot. During the next four years, Confederate Forces occupied the Alamo. A story is told that boys smoking set the roof of the church on fire during the Civil War, but no details or sources are available.

Recollections of an Alamo Guard
Charles T. Smith

Charles T. Smith, a veteran of the Confederacy, was interviewed by the San Antonio <u>Express</u> newspaper in 1917, during the First World War. He stated he stood guard at the Alamo as part of Capt. Bill Edgar's "Alamo Guards."

"When asked if the Alamo appeared any different during the Civil War than it does now, Mr. Smith said, "Yes, there were some changes. For instance, at that time there were outside steps which led up the center of the building to the second floor. The steps ended in a platform. That platform was one of the old slave markets where Negroes were put up at auction. A stout, hardy Negro brought anywhere from $1,000 to $1,500. The thin ones were not rated so high. Men brought bigger prices than women and boys because they could pick more cotton."

Photo of the Alamo Circa 1861.
Note cannon in foreground.   DRT.

Alamo Church & Plaza

Charles T. Smith and the cannon he helped burst. Same cannon as in oval photo.

San Antonio Express/News 1917.

Old Alamo Cannon Broken Open for Treasure

"Talking about being with Captain Edgar's company makes me think of the time we boys tried to burst an old cannon which stood at the west end of that long building I spoke of a few minutes ago. It was a relic of San Jacinto days, which had been dug up and placed there. The muzzle of it was full of spikes. We boys imagined it was full of gold and set to work to get it open. We worked with a sledge hammer for some time, but that was not effective. A woman told us to pour acid over it then to saw it with a yarn string. Of course, we did as we were advised. We kept up the work for days, taking turns about doing the sawing. After we had made a dent a half-inch deep all around the cannon we decided to try the sledge hammer again, and were successful in breaking it open a little above the joint we had been laboring on. There was nothing in the old thing but empty cartridges, and our idea of getting rich that way faded away. That old cannon is now out in San Pedro Springs, in front of that Indian fort. The indentation which we made with that yarn string is still there. I am the only one of the boys living that did that piece of work."

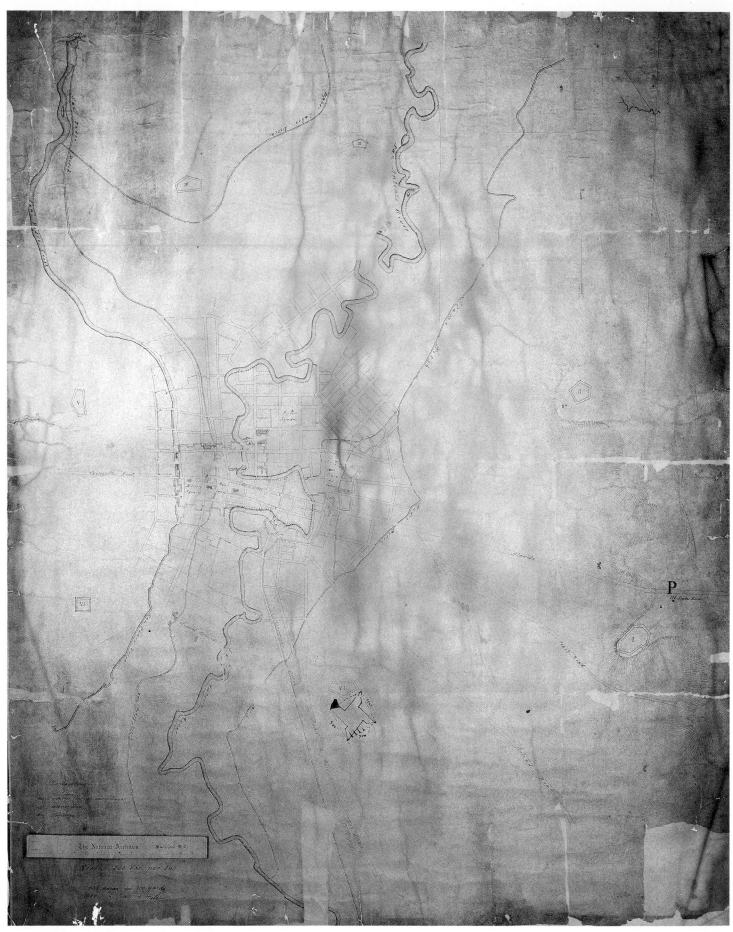

Map of San Antonio during the Civil War showing proposed earthwork forts surrounding the town; **P** denotes powderhouse (La Garita), old Spanish outpost east of Alamo.

Confederate plans to fortify San Antonio

Maps were made during the Civil War that record elaborate plans to encircle San Antonio with an outer ring of earthwork forts and an inner ring of zigzag trenches and picket lines. Sam Maverick complained that few local men were showing up to work on these massive projects. The amount of completion of the trenches and outer forts is not known.

Post-Civil War Return of the U.S. Army

During Reconstruction, the US Army moved back into the Alamo, adding a wagon scale in a pit in front of the church; a new roof may have been built on the church. A new Army base called Ft. Sam Houston was built northwest of the Alamo on a hilltop, around 1879, and the Army moved out of the Alamo. Until then, US Army Headquarters occupied a building erected by Maverick in 1875, at the corner of Alamo Plaza and Houston Street.

Photo ca. 1880, by N.H. Roseca. Note: Markethouse in foreground with new awning. In background is the newly remodeled Grenet Store with elaborate porches, battlements, and towers inclosing the old Convento. New trolley tracks are seen at left. ITC.

FALL OF THE ALAMO

Theodore Gentlitz' reconstruction of the Battle of the Alamo made from the same angle as the above photograph about the same time. In left foreground, the artist reconstructed the Galera demolished in 1871. The Convento does not match earlier drawings. The background showing the terrain seems to be fairly accurate. The original painting was destroyed by fire. DRT.

View of Alamo Plaza, looking north, late 1880's, showing development in the form of extended trolley tracks. Note: Utility pole in foreground. The Markethouse was demolished and the unpaved Plaza was described as a mudhole when it rained. ITC.

1871 - The Demolition of the Old Galera

The old Spanish barrack, gate, and jail complex called the "Galera" ran east-west and formed the south end of the Alamo Plaza was considered old and in the way. The city began to demolish it in 1866. However, the Catholic Church claimed the site and stopped the demolition. As always the case with the Alamo, a controversy developed and the buildings were left as a partial ruin until March 7, 1869, when the San Antonio <u>Daily Express</u> renewed the call for demolition. A pond formed in front of the galera after heavy rains(likely caused by the old filled-in earthwork that protected the main gate in 1836). Finally, in 1871, the city bought the galera from the chruch for $2,500, with the clause that it be demolished and Alamo Plaza and Plaza de Valero be enjoyed as open space for all time.

1876 - A demonstration of the new barbed wire was given by "Bet a Million" Gates in Alamo Plaza. This demonstration led to the widespread use of barbed wire in Texas, ending the open range. A corral of posts and barbed wire was built in the Plaza and a herd of longhorns were driven in, demonstrating how the wire could control the wildest of cattle.

The Grenet Store Takes Over the Alamo

In 1877, a Frenchman named Honore Grenet bought the Convento building and courtyard from the Catholic Church for $20,000. He undertook an elaborate remodeling which included a two-story porch on the west and south side, three wooden towers with wooden fake cannons, and an enclosed courtyard on the east. He operated a museum and a grocery store which also sold wine and liquor.

Hugo Schmeltzer store ca. 1880's. The new owners took over from Grenet in 1884. Note: Only one tower remains with wooden cannons.

ALAMO PLAZA, SAN ANTONIO, TEX.

Alamo Plaza ca. 1890's. Note: Mesquite block paving. New Opera House at left. At center, is new Post Office, with flag. The Alamo is at right.

Frank Celis Postcard Collection, DRT.

The Alamo ca. 1910. Convento building shown with porches removed. Large framework behind may be an electric billboard. ITC.

Alamo ca. 1912, looking northeast. Convento in state of demolition. Center for American History, UT Austin.

Alamo decorated for a celebration in 1890s.   San Antonio Conservation Society, ITC.

1878 - Alamo Plaza Gets a Street Car

A railway running from the old markethouse in Plaza de Valero to San Pedro Springs is built by the city. In 1882, the markethouse is demolished.

1883 - Alamo Church Saved by the State of Texas

On May 16, 1883, the State of Texas pays the Catholic Chruch $20,000 for the old Alamo Church, taking the first step in historical preservation of the Alamo.

1886 - The Grenet Store is sold to Hugo and Schmeltzer Company for $28,000. The Grand Opera House is completed in 1886, located across the Plaza to the west of the corner of Crockett Street.

1887 - The city builds two public water closets and privies on the Plaza.

1888-89 - Alamo Plaza is paved with mesquite wood blocks and property owners facing the Plaza are required to build "Class A" sidewalks in front of their lots. A pipeline is built to the Plaza for the fountain; old photos show a fountain in front of the Hugo-Schmeltzer Store with a classical Greek statue of a woman.

Alamo and Valero Plazas often are described as mud holes after rain. Mesquite blocks are cut into hexagons and placed, end grain up. Later, asphalt paving is placed over these blocks.

1889 - The city condemns the Hugo-Schmeltzer building.

1890 - A new Post Office is completed on the north end of Alamo Plaza.

1891 - A park is laid out in old Plaza de Valero. Trees, shrubs, rosebushes, curbs, and walkways are added. Progress and developement change the Plaza's atmosphere from simple and rustic to a more modern, urban setting as the Twentieth Century approaches.

Feuds Over Preservation of the Convento

In 1893, Adina DeZavala and others formed the DeZavala Chapter of the Daughters of the Republic of Texas and begin efforts to protect the old Spanish Missions along the San Antonio River. Around 1902, she persuades Gustav Schmeltzer to give her historical group first option to buy the old convent building which he owns and uses for a grocery store. In 1903, a hotel syndicate offers to buy the site and build a hotel on the spot. DeZavala went to Clara Driscoll, a young lady of wealth, who, in 1904, put up $500 to Hugo and Schmeltzer with an option to buy the property for $75,000 over four years. Over the next few years, Driscoll put up about $65,000 as private donations came to less than $10,000. Governor S. W. T. Lanham signed legislation on January 26, 1905, for state funding to reimburse Driscoll and on October 4, 1905, conveyed custody of the church and convento property to the Daughters of the Republic of Texas (DRT).

DeZavala and Driscoll fell out over how to develop the site. Driscoll wanted the second story of the old convent demolished as it distracted from the church, which she thought was more important. Adina DeZavala, in protest to save the upper wall, barricaded herself in the old convent after she claimed agents of the hotel syndicate ejected her watchmen. When the law came to order her out, she stopped up her ears with her fingers.

After a three day standoff, she came out. However, in 1913, Governor Oscar Colquitt, who wanted the second floor walls preserved, was out of state and Lt. Gov. Will Mayes supported the Driscoll faction and ordered the upper walls demolished. Gov. Colquitt became embroiled in an acrimonious feud with the DRT, played out in the newspapers for some time.

"San Antonio (the Alamo), Texas, during flower battle, 1896." DRT.

Texas Under Six Flags, ca. 1907 This painting appears to show the Alamo Church decorated with electric lights at night.

From Frank Celis Postcard Collection DRT Library.

"Ruins of the old Alamo and Post Office, San Antonio, Texas."   DRT Library.
This photo creates a panorama when combined with the photo on the right. The old Convento is shown in a state of demolition.

President Taft at the Alamo, 1909. Post Office at left. The porches of the old Convento are gone and dignitaries sit on a temporary platform,

President Roosevelt speaking to an immense crowd on front of Historic Aalamo, San Antonio, Texas.

Note: Billboards above the porches of the old Convento. Many Presidents used the Alamo as a setting for political rallies over the years. In this case, it was Pres. Teddy Roosevelt, ca. 1904.   Postcard collection, DRT Library.

covered with bunting. Alamo Church is partially obscured at right.   From the Leo M.J. Dielmann Papers, DRT Library.

Alamo Plaza, ca. 1910, looking south from the upper floor of the post office. Hugo-Schmeltzer Store is at left. Hotel Alamo is at right. Note: Small fountain in foreground with classical female statute, now gone.
Photo by Lewison's Studio, Robert M. Ayers Estate, ITC.

Convento with porches, removed, looking southeast, ca. 1911.
Coppini Collection, DRT Library.

The Alamo and Fort and Menger Hotel, San Antonio, Tex.

View from Post Office looking southeast. Convento in state of demolition, ca. 1912-13.

Center for American History, UT Austin.

Alamo with wooden derrick in front, ca. 1920, apparently part of construction of new vaulted cement roof.

DRT.

"Ruins of the old Alamo and Post Office" postcard ca. 1912. Combined with photo on right, forms panorama of Alamo Plaza. DRT.

Panoramic view of backside of Convento during demolition looking west. Alamo church, on left, Convento courtyard wall foundation in foreground.

Alamo ca. 1912 Convento shown in a state of demolition. Note: blinded Arches on first floor behind telephone pole. At this stage of the Alamo's condition, a controversy developed between Gov. Colquitt and the DRT, within the DRT, between the De Zavala and Driscoll factions on how to proceed with the protection and reconstruction of the Convento.   Coppini Collection, DRT Library.

Maverick building, with porches, shown above Convento ruins. Post Office at far right.   ITC.

Inside Convento courtyard, ca. 1911 looking south, showing old Hugo Schmeltzer's store at beginning of demolition.   DRT Library.

The Alamo at San Antonio. Texas.

Nov. 22 1848

Northside of Church, 1848 drawing by Seth Eastman, showing inside of Convento courtyard. Point of view is similar to above photos. Note: outhouse and picket fence to left of Church. On horizon above outhouse is La Garita (Powder House).   McNay Art Museum.

Inside Convento courtyard, ca. 1911 looking south, showing old Hugo Schmeltzer's store during demolition. DRT Library.

'54. Ruins of the Historical Alamo, owned by the Daughters of the Republic, San Antonio, Texas

Photo ca. 1912 of inside wall of Convento during demolition, looking south. Similar to above photo after wooden structure removed.
Center for American History, UT Austin.

Bad Ideas that Fortunately were Never Built

The architectural drawings below and to the right were designed by English born architect, Alfred Giles.

THE ALAMO FORT   Copyright, 1908, by Adina De Zavala   THE CHAPEL

Adina De Zavala championed the cause of Alamo preservation, but proposed this totally inaccurate reconstruction of the Convento architectural design using elements borrowed from Mission San Jose.   Center for American History UT Austin.

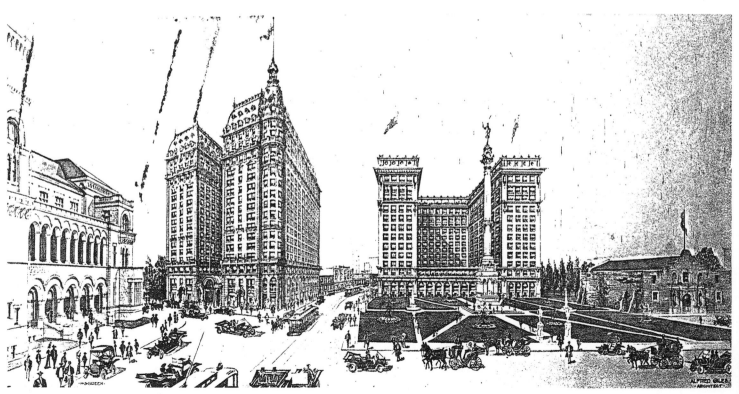

Design for Alamo Plaza with Convento removed and Beaux Arts style building proposed with a more modest monument.

Gov. Colquitt file, Texas State Archives.

COPYRIGHTED 1912 by A.A. BRACK

The Alamo Heroes Monument was to be 802 feet tall. Note: the Alamo Church at lower left.

DRT.

Alamo Plaza ca. 1918

View from Post Office ca. 1916. Fiesta-carnival stalls in Plaza.

ITC.

Return of the Doughboys, ca. 1918-19, at a celebratory watermelon feast at Alamo Plaza.

Photo of second floor, Alamo Church, ca. 1892, built by US Army in 1850. Note: wooden framework of gabled roof. Plate from San Antonio Illustrated, DRT Library.

Interior of the Alamo Church after second floor removed, looking east. San Antonio Conservation Society.

Inside Alamo Church, display cases have been added.

San Antonio <u>Express/News</u> Collection ITC.

Interior of Alamo Church with new cement vaulted roof, ca. 1930.

San Antonio <u>Express-News</u> Collection, ITC.

June 11, 1936, President Franklin Roosevelt visits the Alamo celebrating the Texas Centennial.

1930's view west of Alamo Plaza showing demolition of buildings behind Church for gardens.

1929 Photo, same view as below, fifty years earlier.
1979 Photo of Alamo, center, taken from Tower Life Building.

Atlee B. Ayers Collection, ITC.
Photo by George Nelson, 1979.

Archaeology at Alamo Plaza

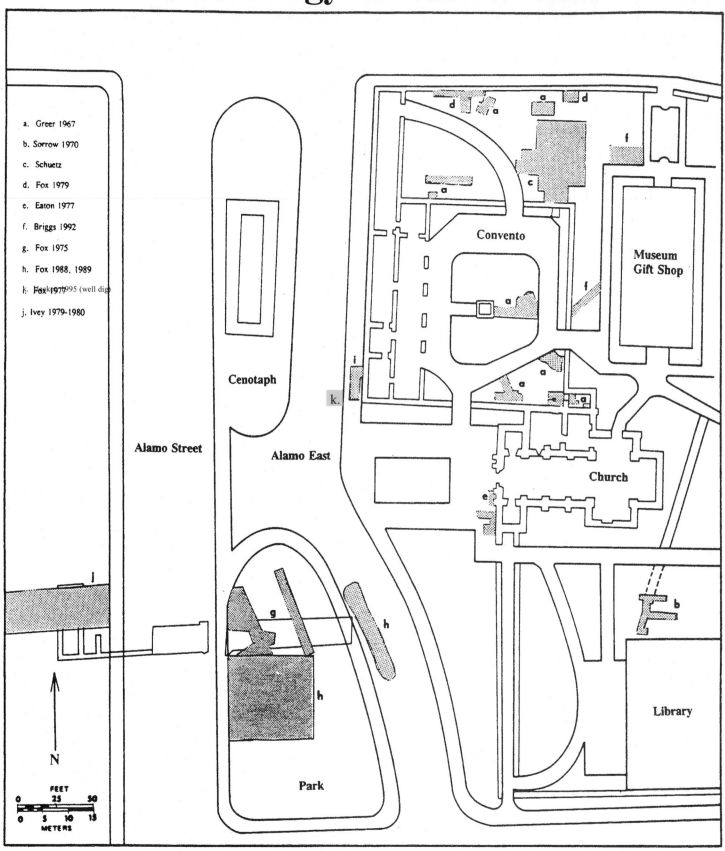

a. Greer 1967

b. Sorrow 1970

c. Schuetz

d. Fox 1979

e. Eaton 1977

f. Briggs 1992

g. Fox 1975

h. Fox 1988, 1989

k. Fox 1995 (well dig)

j. Ivey 1979-1980

Alamo Street

Cenotaph

Alamo East

Convento

Museum Gift Shop

Church

Library

Park

N

FEET
0   25   50
0   5   10   15
METERS

During the past two hundred and fifty years, many excavations were done around Alamo Plaza. Since 1967, careful scientific archaeology has been carried out. This map shows the locations of the various archaeological excavations around Alamo Plaza with the year conducted. This map is taken from, "A Historical Overview of Alamo Plaza and Campo Santo," by The Center for Archaeological Research, UTSA, Robert J. Hard, editor, 1994. The overview was updated in 1995 by the addition of (K), the unsuccessful excavation attempt to locate the well used during the siege of the Alamo.

The Lunette at the Main Gate of the Alamo

A lunette is a crescent-shaped projecting earthwork. At the time of the Battle of the Alamo, it was known that there was a half-moon shaped entrenchment defending the main gate, but the shape and size was unknown until the archeological excavations of 1988. The maps, made in 1836 by Jose Sanchez-Navarro, accurately showed the feature.

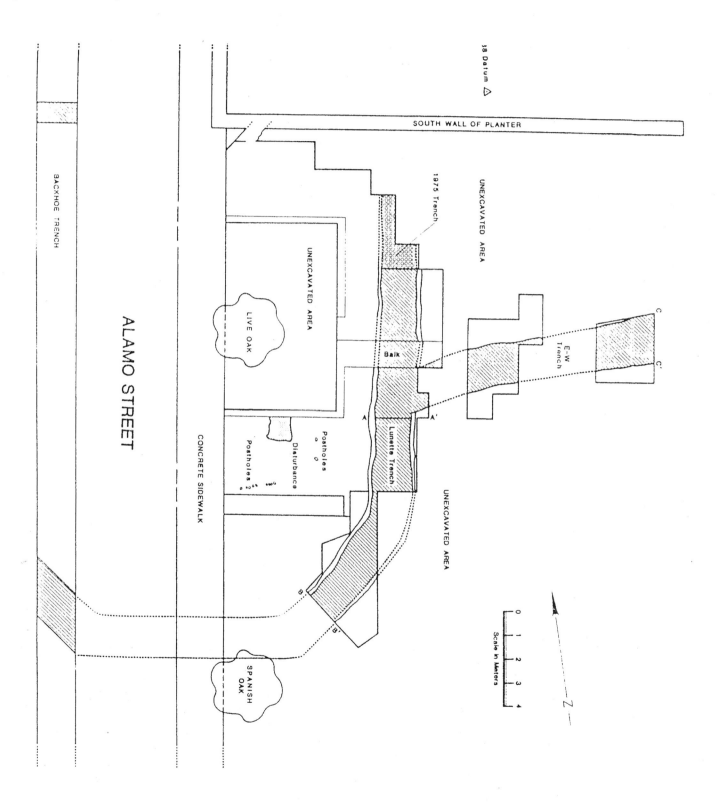

Map of Excavations of the Lunette (half-moon earthwork) outside Alamo Main Gate. Plan of the 1988 excavations. (H) Hatchured areas indicate trenches revealed within excavation.

CAR - UTSA.

Artifacts from Alamo Plaza
San Antonio, Texas

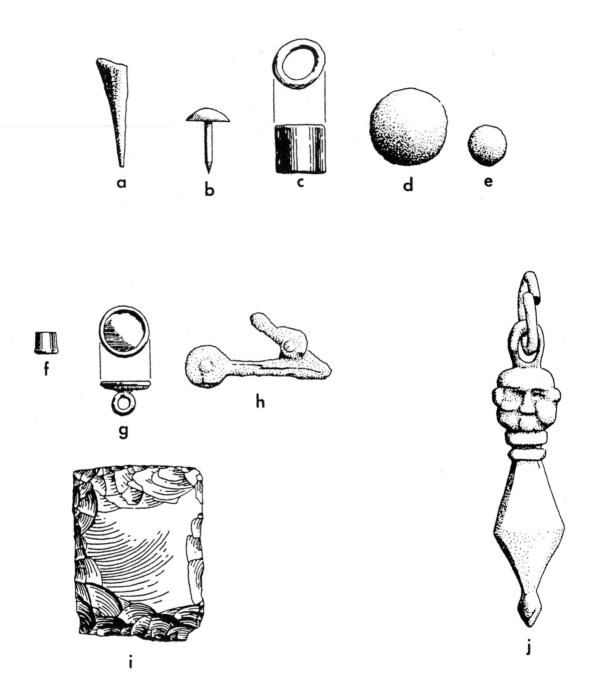

a. pointed fragment of brass; b. copper tack; c. brass ferrule or bead; d. lead musket ball, .68 inch diameter; e. lead pistol or rifle ball, .35 inch diameter; f. percussion cap, brass; g. brass sleeve button; h. sear spring from flintlock rifle; i. musket flint made of local stone; j. brass drawer of cupboard pull, (from Fox, Bass, and Hester 1976: Fig. 26. Courtesy Center for Archaeological Research, The University of Texas at San Antonio, Drawings by D.E. Fox.)

Bibliography

The following is a selected list of works for further reading organized by time periods. Bibliographies in many of these volumes will indicate the direction in which more comprehensive studies may be undertaken.

Major Collections

Bexar Archives (1718-1836).
Center for American History, University of Texas at Austin.
Center for Archaeological Research, UTSA.
D.R.T. Library, The Alamo, San Antonio, TX.
National Archives, Washington, D.C.
Old Mission Research Library, Our Lady of the Lake University, San Antonio, TX.
Texas State Library,Texas Army Papers, Austin, TX.

Prehistoric Background

Campbell, T.N., The Payaya Indians of Southern Texas, Special Pub. Southern Texas Archaeological Assn., 1975.

Hester, Thomas R. Digging Into South Texas Prehistory, Corona Publishing Co., San Antonio, TX, 1980.

Stothert, Karen E., The Archaeology and Early History of the Head of the San Antonio River, Special publication No. 5 and Incarnate Word College Archaeology Series No. 3, San Antonio, TX.

Early Spanish Exploration

Castaneda, Carlos, Our Catholic Heritage, Vol I-II, Texas Knights of Columbus Historical Committee. Von Boeckman-Jones, Austin, TX, 1936.

A.J. McGraw, John W. Clark, and Elizabeth A. Robbins, editors. A Texas Legacy, the Old San Antonio Road and the Camino Reales, A Tri-Centennial History, 1691-1991, Texas Department of Highways and Public Transportation, Austin TX, 1991.

Spanish Mission Period

Bexar Archives, (1718-1836), Center for American History, UT Austin.

Castaneda, Carlos, Our Catholic Heritage in Texas, Vol. II-V, Von Boeckman-Jones Co., Austin, TX, 1939.

De la Teja, Jesus F., San Antonio de Bexar, A Community on New Spain's Northern Frontier, University of New Mexico, Albuquerque, 1995.

Habig, Fr. Marion, OFM The Alamo Mission: San Antonio de Valero 1718-1793, Franciscan Herald Press, Chicago, IL, 1977.

Heusinger, Edward, A Chronology of Events in San Antonio, Standard Printing, San Antonio, TX.

Tunnel, Curtis, Series Editor, Inventory of the Mission San Antonio de Valero, 1772, Texas Historical Commission, Special Report #23, 1977.

Valero Becomes the Alamo

Castaneda, Carlos, Our Catholic Heritage in Texas, (see above), Vol. VI.,

Bexar Archives, The University of Texas at Austin.

Nixon, Pat, A Century of Medicine in San Antonio, San Antonio, TX, 1936.

Robert H. Thornhoff, editor and annotator, Forgotten Battlefield of the First Texas Revolution, Eakin Press, Austin, TX, 1985.

The Texas Revolution

Andrade, Juan, Documentos De El Gen. Andrade, Publica sobre La evacuation de la ciudad de San Antonio de Bejar, del Dept. Of Tejas, Editora Nacional, S.A. Mexico, DF, 1952 (collection of Kevin Young, Translated by Dora Guerra).

Dr. J.H. Barnard's Journal, Goliad Bicentennial Edition, 1949.

Brown, Gary, The New Orleans Greys, Republic of Texas Press, 1999

Castaneda., Carlos, translator and editor, The Mexican Side of the Texas Revolution, Arno Press 1976, New York, NY.

de La Pena, Jose Enrique, With Santa Ana in Texas, translated and edited by Carmen Perry, Texas A&M Press, College Station, TX, 1975.

Ehrenberg, Herman, With Milam and Fannin, Pemberton Press, Austin, TX, 1968.

Filisola, Vincente, Memoirs For the History of the War In Texas, 1849, Vol 2., trans. by Wallack Woolsey, Eakin Press, Austin, TX, 1952.

Green, Rena Maverick, Samuel Maverick, Texas, privately published, San Antonio, TX, 1952.

Hardin, Stephen L., Texian Iliad, A Military History of the Texas Revolution, 1835-36, U.T. Press, Austin, TX, 1994.

Huffines, Allen, The Siege and Battle of the Alamo, an Illustrated Chronology, Eakin Press, Austin, TX, 1999.

Jenkins, John J. ed, The Papers of the Texas Revolution-1835-36, Vol 10, Presidial Press, Austin, TX, 1973.

Long, Jeff, Duel of Eagles, the Mexican and U.S. Fight For the Alamo, N.Y., 1990.

Lord, Walter, A Time to Stand, Harper & Bro., NY., 1961.

Matovina, Timothy, The Alamo Remembered, UT Press 1995.

Potter, Reuben M., The Fall of the Alamo - 1878, (reprint), Hillsdale, NJ, Otterdes Press, 1977.

Sanchez-Navarro, Carlos, La Guerra de Tejas, Mexico City, 1938.

Texas Army Papers, Texas State Library.

Tinkle, Lon, Thirteen Days to Glory, NY, 1958.

Williams, Amelia, A Critical Study of the Siege of the Alamo and the Personnel of its Defenders, Ph.D. diss., U.T. At Austin, 1931, Southwestern Historical Quarterly, Vol. 36.

The Republic of Texas

Bollaert, William, William Bollaert's Texas, The University of Oklahoma Press, Norman, OK, 1956.

Carroll, J. M., History of the Texas Baptists, Baptist Standard, 1923, pp. 184.

Maverick Papers, Center for American History, UT Austin.

Nance, Joseph M., Attack and Counter-Attack, UT Press, Austin, TX, 1965.

Pierce, Gerald S., Texas Under Arms, The Camps, Post, Forts and Military Towns of the Republic of Texas 1836-46, Encino Press, Austin, TX 1969.

U.S. Army Occupation of the Alamo

Casteneda, Carlos, Our Catholic Heritage in Texas, supplement, The Vicariate, 1841-47.

Records of the War Department, Office of the Quartermaster Gen. Consolidated File, National Archives, Washington, D.C.

Ahlborn, Richard Eighme, The San Antonio Mission and the American Occupation, 1847, Amon Carter Museum, Ft. Worth, TX.

Edward, Everett, Transactions of the Illinois Historical Society for the year 1905-06, narrative, Part III, pp. 210-29.

Handy, Mary Oliva, History of Ft. Sam Houston, Naylor Co., 1951, San Antonio, TX.

The Civil War

The War of Rebellion, A Compilation of Official Records of the Union and Confederate Armies, Series I, Vol. 1, Washington Government Printing Office, 1880.

Merrick, Morgan W., From Desert to Bayou, UT El Paso, Texas Western Press.

Young, Kevin, To The Tyrants Never Yield, a Texas Civil War Sampler, Wondware Press, Plano, TX. 1992.

Sprague, Major J.T., Treachery in Texas, New York Historical Society, 1862.

Smith, Charles T., "56 Years and the Alamo Again Sees the Boys March to the Front," San Antonio Express-News, 1917.

Williams, J.R., With the Border Ruffians, Dutton, New York.

The Twentieth Century

The Post-Civil War history of the Alamo is mainly covered by photographs in this book; however, the following sources deal with this period.

Texas State Library, Archives Division, Gov. Oscar Colquitt file.

Brear, Holly Beachley, Inherit the Alamo, Myth and Ritual at an American Shrine, UT Press, Austin.

De Zavala, Adina, History and Legends of the Alamo and Other Missions in and Around the San Antonio Area, republished and edited by Richard Flores, Original publication date 1917, Arte Publico Press, Houston, TX 1997.

Jennings, Frank W., "Adina DeZavala, Alamo Crusader," Texas Highway Magazine, March, 1995.

Schoelwer, Susan Pendergast with Tom W. Glaser, Alamo Images: Changing Perceptions of a Texas Experience, DeGolyer Library and S.M.U. Press, Dallas, TX, 1985.

Archaeological Reports

Eaton, Jack D, Excavations at the Alamo Shrine (Mission San Antonio de Valero), Special Report No. 10, C.A.R., UTSA, San Antonio, TX, 1980.

Fox, Anne A., F. Bass and Thomas Hester, The Archaeology and History of Alamo Plaza, Report No. 16, Center for Archaeological Research, UTSA, San Antonio, TX, 1976.

Fox, Anne A., Archaeological and Historical Investigations at the Alamo North Wall, UTSA, C.A.R. 1980.

Fox, Anne A., Archaeological Investigations in Alamo Plaza 1988-89, Report No. 205, C.A.R., UTSA, 1992.

Green, J. W., A Description of The Stratigraphy, Features and Artifacts from an Archaeological Excavation at the Alamo, Report No. 4., Texas State Building Commission, 1967.

Hard, Robert, Editor, A Historical Overview of the Alamo and Campo Santo, C.A.R., Special Report No. 20, 1994.

Ivey, Jake, Unpublished Manuscripts, file at the C.A.R., UTSA.

Schuetz, M. K. Archaeological Investigations at Mission San Antonio de Valero, Second Patio,

Sorrow, W. M., Archaeological Salvage Excavations at the Alamo, T.A.S. Report No. 4, Austin, TX 1972.

Uecker, Herbert, Interim Report, 1995 Alamo Wells Project St. Mary's University Archaeology Program.

Alamo Defenders and Their Place of Origin

The following list of names is taken from a list compiled by the Daughters of the Republic of Texas and other sources. Unfortunately, no official list of names survives from 1836. The following list was assembled from various sources such as land bounty records, military unit records, and memories of various individuals and likely omits some defenders. The abbreviation 'NOG' next to the names refers to New Orleans Greys, a group of volunteers. When this book was started decades ago, the list numbered 182 men; the list grew to 189. Some Mexican sources state that about 254-7 defenders were killed. The question remains: "How many native Texans (Tejanos) were killed?" Modern lists claim six or eight, but Travis, in his last letter, states only three were in the Fort. (see p. 48) (This list is meant for general reference only.)

Texas 8
Abamillo, Juan
Espalier, Carlos
Esparza, Gregorio
Fuentes, Antonio
Guerrero, Jose Maria
Jimenes (Ximenes) Damacio
Losoya, Toribio
Nava, Andres

Tennessee 30
Bayliss, Joseph
Blair, John
Blair, Samuel
Bowman, Jesse B.
Campbell, Robert
Crockett, David
Daymon, Squire
Dearduff, William
Dickinson, Almeron
Dillard, John Henry
Garrett, James Girard (NOG)
Harrison, Andrew Jackson
Hays, John M.
Heiskell, Charles M.
Hutchinson, T.P. (NOG)
Marshall, William (NOG)
McCoy, Jesse
McKinney, Robert
Miller, William
Mills, William
Nelson, Andrew M.
Robertson, James Waters
Summerlin, S. Spain
Summers, William E.
Taylor, Edward
Taylor, George
Taylor, James
Taylor, William
Walker, Asa
Walker, Jacob

Kentucky 16
Bailey, Peter James, III
Bowie, James
Cloud, Damiel William
Darst, Jacob C.
Davis, John
Fauntleroy, William Keener
Gaston, John E.
Harris, John
Jackson, William Daniel
Jameson, Green B.
Kellog, John Benjamin

Kent, Andrew
Rutherford, Joseph
Thomas, B. Archer M.
Washington, Joseph G.
White, Issac (or Alabama)

Virginia 12
Allen, Robert
Baugh, John J. (NOG)
Carey, William R.
Goodrich, John C.
Herndon, Patrick Henry
Kenney, James
Lewis, William Irvine
Lightfoot, William J.
Main, George Washington (NOG)
Mitchusson, Edward F.
Moore, Robert B. (NOG)
Northcross, James

Pennsylvania 15
Ballentine, John
Brown, James
Cain, John
Crossman, Robert
Cummings, David P.
Hannum, James
Holloway, Samuel (NOG)
Jennings, Gordon C.
Johnson, William
Kimbell, George C.
McDowell, William
Reynolds, John Purdy
Thruston, John M.
Williamson, Hyram James
Wilson, John

South Carolina 7
Bonham, James Butler
Crawford, Lemuel
Neegan, George
Nelson, Edward
Nelson, George (NOG)
Simmons, Cleveland
Travis, William Barrett

Georgia 5
Grimes, Albert Calvin
Malone, William T.
Melton, Eliel
Shied, Manson
Wells, William

Missouri 6
Baker, William Charles M.
Butler, George D.
Clark, Charles Henry (NOG)
Cottle, George Washington
Day, Jerry C.

Tumlinson, George W.

New York 6
Cunningham, Robert
Dewall, Lewis
Evans, Samuel B.
Forsyth, John Hubbard
Jones, John (NOG)
Tylee, James

Alabama 3
Buchanan, James
Fuqua, Galba
White, Issac (or Kentucky)

Louisiana 4
Despallier, Charles (NOG)
Garrand, James W.
Kerr, Joseph
Ryan, Issac

Massachusetts 4
Flanders, John
Howell, William D. (NOG)
Linn, William (NOG)
Pollard, Amos

Ohio 4
Harrison, William B.
Holland, Tarpley
Musselman, Robert
Rose, James M.

Mississppi 3
Clark, M.B.
Millsaps, Issac
Moore, Willis A.

Arkansas 2
Baker, Issac G.
Thompson, Jesse G.

Conneticut 1
(name unavailable)

Illinios 1
Lindley, Jonathan L.

Maryland 1
Smith, Charles S.

New Hampshire 1
Cochran, Robert E

New Jersey 1
Stockton, Richard L.

Rhode Island 1
Martin, Albert

Vermont 1
Andross, Miles DeForrest

European

England 12
Blazeby, William (NOG)
Bourne, Daniel
Brown, George
Dennison, Steph. (NOG)(or Ireland)

Dimpkins, James R.
Gwynne, James C.
Hersee, William Daniel (NOG)
Nowlan, James
Sewell Marcus L.
Starr, Richard (NOG)
Stewart, James E.
Waters, Thomas (NOG)

Ireland 12
Burns, Samuel E.
Dennison, Stephen (NOG)
(or England)
Duvalt, Andrew
Evans, Robert
Hawkins, Joseph M.
Jackson, Thomas
McGee, James (NOG)
Mormon, John (NOG)
Rusk, Jackson J.
Spratt, John (NOG)
Trammel, Burke
Ward, William B.

Scotland 4
Ballantine, Richard W.
McGregor, John
Robinson, Issac
Wilson, David L.

Germany 2
Courtman, Henry (NOG)
Thomas, Henry (NOG)

Wales 1
Johnson, Lewis

Denmark 1
Zanco, Charles

Unknown Place of Origin
Brown, Robert
Day, Freeman H.K.
Fishbaugh, William
Garvin, John E.
George, James
King, William Philip
McCaffery, Edward
Mitchell, Edwin T.
Mitchell, Napoleon B.
Pagan, George
Parker, Christopher Adam
Richardson, Perry
Roberts, Thomas H.
Smith, Andrew H.
Smith William H.
Sutherland, William De Priest
Warnell, Henry
Wills, William
Wolf, Anthony

Indian Tribes Represented at Mission Valero 1718-1793

Mission Valero Records include lists of births, marriages, and deaths. Around one thousand mission Indians were buried during the Mission Period.

Apache	Pacuache
Lipan Apache	Paizala
Apion	Pallugam
Aponpia	Pamaia
Caguia	Papanaque
Capuas	Paquache
Caxancaques	Pasojo
Cenisot	Pataqua
Chana	Pauihan
Charame	Payaya
Chana	Pazan
Coco	Penaca
Copan	Pomaia
Fumse	Punctagu
Guimen	Quems
Hacona	Sana
Haipocasa	Senizo
Hierbipiamo	Siaguan
Iman	Sifame
Ipandi	Tancaque
Janacaz	Taroname
Jumana	Timeamar
Junayai	Tou
Juxzan	Tucame
Masuan	Yechipian
Mecocame	Yijame
Mesquite	Yojuan
Moruame	Xarane
Nonopho	Zacpoco
Oreoguese	Ziapuan
Orejan	Zolajan
Pactan	

INDEX

INDEX (cont.)